ESSENTIAL BELIEFS

a wesleyan primer

Mark A. Maddix
&
Diane Leclerc

Editors

BEACON HILL PRESS
OF KANSAS CITY

Beacon Hill Press of Kansas City
PO Box 419527
Kansas City, MO 64141
beaconhillbooks.com
ISBN 978-0-8341-3570-3

Printed in the
United States of America

Cover Design: J.R. Caines
Interior Design: Sharon Page

Library of Congress Cataloging-in-Publication Data
Names: Maddix, Mark A., 1965- editor. | Leclerc, Diane, 1963- editor.
Title: Essential beliefs : a Wesleyan primer / Mark A. Maddix and Diane Leclerc, editors.
Description: Kansas City, MO : Beacon Hill Press of Kansas City, 2016. |
    Includes bibliographical references.
Identifiers: LCCN 2016021088 | ISBN 9780834135703 (pbk.)
Subjects: LCSH: Theology, Doctrinal—Popular works.
Classification: LCC BT77 .E685 2016 | DDC 230/.7—dc23 LC record available at https://lccn.loc.gov
/2016021088

The internet addresses, email addresses, and phone numbers in this book are accurate at the time of publication. They are provided as a resource. Beacon Hill Press of Kansas City does not endorse them or vouch for their content or permanence.

10 9 8 7 6 5 4 3 2 1

CONTENTS

INTRODUCTION
THEOLOGY IN OVERALLS

—◊◊◊—

Mark A. Maddix and Diane Leclerc

This is a book about God. The Greek words that refer to the study of God are *theos*, meaning God, and *logos*, meaning words. From this, we get the word *theology*. So, literally, theology is God talk. This is a theology book. But unlike many theology books, this one is geared toward laypeople—those who are not formally trained in theology, as are pastors and professors. J. Kenneth Grider once said, "Theology must fit into overalls!" We find his words compelling, and take them as a guide. Theology is not worth a lick if it cannot be made clear to the people in the pews, on the farm, or in a sophomore college classroom. We have tried hard as editors to make this book understandable and easy to use for those who want to know and appreciate the essential beliefs of the Christian faith, particularly from a Wesleyan-holiness perspective.

We strongly believe that this book is needed, in light of the fact that there is much concern and confusion about "right" theology today. There seems to be a great deal of anxiety about theology. *Theology* is often a misunderstood word, and some people can even feel threatened by it. Let's put forth an initial definition here: *Theology is the process of taking the grand truth of the scriptural witness to Jesus Christ and applying it to the present-day context.* This definition suggests two ideas. First, there is a stability in theology because it is based on Scripture and the ancient church's interpretation of its message. In this sense, the truth of the message about God, and humanity's relationship with God, is timeless and applicable to all. Second, theology must do the hard work of translating such theological truth into the language and ideas of the present age. In this sense, theology develops. Theology, no matter how truthful, must always be applied. We acknowledge that simple *indoctrination* of the way the truth has been articulated in the past will not be adequate in the present or the future. Truth—as it is in Jesus—does not change, but it is vitally important to communicate the truth in ways understandable to people in other contexts (which could simply include those in younger generations). We the editors believe that the churches of the Wesleyan-holiness family desperately need to know our essential beliefs, and be able to distinguish them from the nonessentials of our theology. It is only as we understand these essentials that we can then translate them in ways that relate to those with whom we want to communicate.

Let's start at the beginning, with the early church. When we think of the early church period, we of course begin with Pentecost, then follow Paul on his missionary journeys, and continue with the writing of the New Testament itself. But sometimes we forget that the Bible was canonized centuries after it was written. In other words, identifying the books that were chosen as holy Christian Scripture, while excluding others, was a lengthy and dynamic process that concluded in the year 367![1] Certain gospels and epistles were certainly recognized as having authority in the church prior to this time, but the closing of the official Canon took a very long while.

In recognizing the reality of the lengthy process of canonization, we need also to appreciate that differing interpretations of Christian truths appeared early in the development of the church, even before the Canon closed. An important aspect of self-identity came as the church began to recognize persons and ideas in their midst that were so off that they really misrepresented the gospel of Jesus Christ. Irenaeus of Lyons was the first to use the word *heresy* (in the latter part of the second century). He was opposed to the teachings of Valentinus, a Gnostic who was leading Christians astray, all the while believing himself to be very much a Christian. Gnostics were wrong about lots of things, including the belief that the body of Jesus was not a real human body. Irenaeus drew a line in the sand and declared that Gnostics stood outside the Christian circle because their beliefs were just too different. This conflict led to the obvious but (up until then) little-acknowledged need of the church to articulate accurately what beliefs where thoroughly Christian. Why were Gnostics heretics? What constituted true Christian faith? Since the Gnostics used the same, yet-to-be-canonized Scripture, on what basis could Christians claim to know the truth? Irenaeus and others began to speak of an "apostolic succession" of teachers as a way of legitimizing Christian doctrine. For example, Irenaeus was taught by Polycarp, who was taught by the apostle John, who was taught by Jesus.

The next major step in determining Christian truth was the development of early Christian creeds that often came from key councils that met to determine extremely important decisions regarding Christian theology. One of the greatest debates in early Christianity was over Christology. There were numerous heresies

---

1. The exact date is hard to pin down. The year 367 is but one of many dates that are given because the exact books we recognize today were listed by an important church father.

about the nature of Jesus Christ through the first five centuries. One debate in particular came to a head in the early 300s.

Arius was an important church leader in Alexandria, Egypt. He came to believe and preach that Christ was "begotten" of the Father, but he interpreted that to mean that there was a time when the second person of the Trinity was *created* by God, and that there was "a time when he was not." A second aspect of his teaching was whether Christ was of the very same essence of the Father, or just *like* God's character. He opted for *like*. Alexander of Alexandria and Athanasius became the proponents of the opposite view on these two points. Emperor Constantine became aware of the divisive debate and called the first ecumenical council at Nicaea in 325. (*Ecumenical* implies that all Christians—Protestant, Catholic, Orthodox—affirm the decisions of these councils. There have been seven ecumenical councils.) It was decided at Nicaea that Arianism was heresy and that Athanasius and Alexander's position should be adopted as the orthodox view of Christ. Christ is coeternal with God, sharing the very same essence. Three other councils followed that are also known as Christological councils. They further fine-tuned the orthodox position on the nature and person of Jesus Christ. Many know the earlier Apostles' Creed. The next important creed of the church is the Nicene Creed:

I believe in one God, the Father Almighty, maker of heaven and earth, and of all things visible and invisible;

And in one Lord Jesus Christ, the only-begotten Son of God, begotten of his Father before all worlds, God of God, Light of Light, very God of very God, begotten, not made, being of one substance with the Father; by whom all things were made; who for us and for our salvation came down from heaven, and was incarnate by the Holy Spirit of the Virgin Mary, and was made man; and was crucified also for us under Pontius Pilate; he suffered and was buried; and the third day he rose again according to the Scriptures, and ascended into heaven, and sits on the right hand of the Father; and he shall come again, with glory, to judge both the living and the dead; whose kingdom shall have no end.

And I believe in the Holy Spirit, the Lord, and Giver of Life, who proceeds from the Father and the Son; who with the Father and the Son together is worshiped and glorified; who spoke by the prophets. And I believe in one holy catholic (universal) and apostolic church; I acknowledge one baptism for the remission of sins; and I look for the resurrection of the dead, and the life of the world to come. Amen.[2]

---

2. Adapted from "The Nicene Creed," in *The Book of Common Prayer* (New York: Church Hymnal Corporation, 1979), 327–28, http://justus.anglican.org/resources/bcp/euchr1.pdf.

It could be said that the Creeds represent the earliest lists of the *essentials* of Christian faith. They represent early interpretations of the Bible and sum up the heart of theology. Since they are still affirmed by all orthodox Christians, they are a good place to start.

But, as history has shown, churches have split over what true doctrine is. We have the same Bible, but we interpret it differently. This is the reality with which we must wrestle. An incorrect way to solve it is to believe that *my*, or even *our*, interpretation is right on everything and that everyone else is completely wrong. But how do we move forward?

The first split of the church happened in 1054 when Eastern Orthodoxy and Roman Catholicism parted ways. The next splits happened during the Protestant Reformation. Since then, more than forty thousand different denominations have developed, each believing, of course, that what they hold to be true is the most correct. But who is right? And how do we know? We are faced with the question of Christian diversity. Christians believe very different things about very important matters. How do we make sense of this?

John Wesley wrote a really important sermon titled "The Catholic Spirit." He tries to make sense of Christian diversity and offers key insights on how to handle it. In sum, he recognizes that we can disagree, even strongly, with other Christians—in fact, it is inevitable; but we must always, always love each other despite our differences over doctrine. Phineas Bresee, the founder of the Church of the Nazarene, echoes Wesley when he affirms, "In essentials unity, in non-essentials liberty, in all things charity."[3] Indeed, love over all. But it is important also to determine what is essential and what is nonessential so that we can be assured that we put first things first and allow other Christians "liberty of thinking" (a Wesley phrase) on secondary issues. All of us are to sincerely seek the truth. Yet the word *truth* in today's secular and religious cultures has taken on very weighty, but very different and opposing meanings.

In the secular realm, truth has become relative and *purely* contextual in this postmodern era. It doesn't matter what people believe, as long as they are true to themselves and don't infringe on other people's rights. In response, the religious world has sometimes felt threatened by a society without boundaries and set value statements. In light of this perceived threat and the understandable anxiety surrounding it, it has become very important to some to set boundaries of doctrine and to press hard to guard and protect *the* truth. But sometimes truth has been pressed into a box or hidden behind fences, so to speak, and has been

---

3. See Mark Maddix, "Understanding the Essentials," *Holiness Today*, November/December 2011; see also *The Nazarene Messenger* 5, no. 23 (Dec. 6, 1900): 4. The actual quote has been attributed to Augustine, although many scholars believe it came much later, perhaps from the Lutheran tradition.

viewed as something not to be explored and gratefully welcomed but fiercely safeguarded and defended. Truth held with this tight, self-protective attitude can be reduced to objective presuppositions that are considered inflexible and absolute.

Wesleyan theology has always attempted to transcend these extreme positions between secular relativism and rigid absolutism. Truth, for Wesley, is primarily embodied and not abstract. Truth is personally discovered and embraced. Specifically, truth *is* the person of Jesus Christ whom we encounter. Thus, when reference is made to seeking *truth* in Wesleyan theology and life, in reality it means nothing more and nothing less than seeking personal engagement with God through Christ as enabled by the Spirit. This does not mean that there are not truths to which we hold. But it does imply, in a Wesleyan-holiness paradigm, that genuine relationship takes precedence over static faith statements and cold, doctrinal propositions. The search for truth, as it is in Jesus, is an adventure. The adventure's goal is the sanctified life.

As Wesley himself says, one can intellectually affirm belief statements, even about Christ, without truly *being* Christian in the world. Indeed, as James says, even the demons *believe* and shudder. When John Wesley explores being Christian, he focuses on "faith filled with the energy of love" being lived out and not held tight.[4] What makes theology Wesleyan is that it seeks not only to be informative but to be formative and transformative through engagement with the living God and with the lost and broken world.

This book is *about* theology; it is a book that *does* theology; and, hopefully, it will prove to be *be* a living, breathing theology. Each chapter in this book is intended to inform the reader about a particular doctrine, but we hope that each chapter can also be a means of transformation toward wholeness. There is much need for the people of the Wesleyan-holiness tradition to understand more clearly what we believe about all of the matters discussed in these chapters. But we also firmly believe that such understanding is also a call to live out what truly *matters* in this life. We are called to holy love. This is the major aim of Wesleyan-holiness theology, and of this book. The love of God is our most important essential.

The book is divided into five parts. Part 1 continues the discussion hinted at here of what it means to do theology. In chapter 1, Dick Eugenio examines theological method, focusing on the Wesleyan inductive approach that is experiential and practical. In other words, he further clarifies that Wesleyan theology is less about abstract thinking and more about the transformation of the whole person in Jesus Christ.

---

4. John Wesley, "Catholic Spirit," in *The Works of John Wesley*, ed. Thomas Jackson, 14 vols. (Kansas City: Beacon Hill Press of Kansas City, 1978), 5:497. Hereinafter abbreviated *Works*.

Celia Wolff, in chapter 2, concentrates on a Wesleyan way to interpret Scripture and how Scripture functions within the life of the church. She emphasizes Wesley's view of the Bible as a guide for Christian faith and practice that shapes and forms people into faithful disciples. She also provides some practical guidelines for how to read the Bible in order to have a Scripture-shaped life.

Part 1 concludes with John Grant's chapter on the Wesleyan quadrilateral as the foremost Wesleyan way of doing theology. For Wesley, Scripture is primary and is supported by the rich heritage of church tradition, our own, God-given reason, and our personal experiences. Grant provides a clear understanding of how interpreters of Scripture are to utilize these sources to understand Scripture for the purpose of applying it to daily life.

After the foundation has been laid for why and how we do theology, the second part of the book focuses on the Trinity. In chapter 4, Tim Gaines centers his discussion on the historical understanding of the Godhead as one essence and three persons. This view reflects the relational communion of the Father, Son, and Holy Spirit as one God.

In chapter 5, Benjamin Cremer provides a clear explanation of Christ's nature as both human and divine. This dynamic of holding together the divine and human natures in the one person of Christ keeps the character of God always before us. Christ shows God's faithful love by coming in the flesh to live among us.

Rhonda Crutcher reminds us in chapter 6 that the Holy Spirit is active in leading, guiding, and interceding for us. For Wesleyans, the Holy Spirit provides assurance and confirmation of salvation and is a dynamic presence who leads Christians on the path toward holiness of heart and life.

A proper understanding of the triune God is critical going into the third part of the book: Creation, Humanity, and Sin. Eric Vail discusses how God creates out of nothing (*creation ex nihilo*). He also talks about the Bible's affirmation of the goodness of God's material creation and the importance of restoring and redeeming it. He connects the gift of creation with God's divine love that invites our cooperation in restoring all things.

Ryan Hansen shows the impact of the fall of humanity and the distortion of the image of God (*imago Dei*); thus, the need for the redemption of Christ to restore humanity's relationship with God. He argues that Wesley's view of the human person is relational.

In chapter 9, Diane Leclerc maintains that the greatest threat to holiness is sin. A Wesleyan understanding of sin is needed to inform a person's faith and practice. She states that sin is always anti-love and that it damages and destroys relationship with God and others. She provides a helpful discussion about Wesley's view of imperfections and infirmities as amoral. She shows the difference between Augustine and Wesley's views of original sin and the role that prevenient grace plays in restoring free will.

In chapter 10, Sarah Whittle addresses a very difficult aspect of theology, systemic evil. Whittle illustrates the impact of systemic evil in economic and political structures that benefit the wealthy and often perpetuate injustice, gender discrimination, racism, and a lust for power. She argues that a Wesleyan view of holiness is both social and corporate: Thus, Christians have a responsibility to guard against the forces that hinder human flourishing.

The last chapter of part 3 addresses the issue of divine theodicy. Joe Gorman shows that God does not *cause* pain and suffering since God is a God of love. He asserts that all persons are fallen and will suffer and that the traditional free will argument, or any argument, doesn't provide final answers to theodicy. He provides a pastoral response to the problem of suffering by affirming that God is present in the midst of pain.

Part 4 answers the questions surrounding salvation, sanctification, ethics, and Christian growth. Jacob Lett concentrates on the person of Jesus Christ and his atoning work. For Wesley, the work of Christ provides reconciliation, new birth, and participation as part of what was done on the cross. It is through the redemption of Christ that individuals are reconciled to God, receive the new birth, and participate in the triune Godhead.

In chapter 13, David McEwan discusses the importance of sanctification. He explains that sanctification is a loving relationship with God and others. McEwan states that restoring relationship with God is not simply about the forgiveness of sin, as important as that is, but it is also about changing the heart's inclination to love creation above the Creator. It is the work of the Holy Spirit through sanctification that re-creates and reshapes this inclination to love God and then neighbor. He continues Leclerc's discussion by reminding us of the limitations of sanctification.

Gift Mtukwa's chapter talks about Wesley's call to reform the nations. He discusses the Wesleyan view of prevenient grace and how humans have agency (free will) and human consciousness as gifts from God. He shows that a Wesleyan ethic includes social holiness and the need to engage in acts of mercy and compassionate stewardship.

In the last chapter of part 4, Mark Maddix explains how we grow spiritually through participation in the Christian practices (inward, outward, and corporate). These practices, or means of grace, open us up to receive God's grace and to form us into Christlikeness.

The final part of the book centers on the meaning, purpose, and hope (ecclesiology) of the church. Montague Williams begins this section affirming that we believe in one, holy, catholic (meaning universal), and apostolic church. He shows that the church consists of Christians worldwide and that its apostolic function is to pass on the teachings and tradition of Jesus's original disciples. The nature of the church has implications for its mission in the world.

In chapter 17, Joshua and Nell Sweeden discuss Wesley's discipleship process of small groups and how he provided a variety of avenues to reach the least, lost, and less fortunate of society. They illustrate that John Wesley and his brother Charles took seriously the idea that the world was their parish through itinerant preaching, small groups, and social justice. The Sweedens make parallels between John Wesley's renewal movement and today's current missional church movement.

Kelly Diehl Yates discusses how we are to view people of other religions. Yates begins by further developing Wesley's view of prevenient grace to show that God calls all persons to Christ, who loves all people. She suggests that Wesleyans should practice humility toward other religions by recognizing that it is the free grace of God that has saved us—rather than anything we've done. She continues by exploring the importance of respecting other religions and practicing kindness toward them.

In the final chapter, Charles Christian provides an overview of several traditional options of eschatology, which he asserts are not Wesleyan. He then provides a Wesleyan alternative by stating that the kingdom of God is here and now, the last days are about a person (Jesus), and God's goal is transformation. He concludes by showing that eschatology is about optimism, not pessimism. Indeed, all of Wesleyan theology is optimistic.

We have asked young theologians, or theologians from other cultures, to write for us. As we move into a new century, a living theology such as Wesleyan-holiness theology needs to be expressed for all to hear, but especially in ways accessible to newer generations and other cultures. Most, if not all, of the contributions to this book share a common theological language and common themes, and all are insightfully and creatively articulated. It is our prayer that this primer on our essential beliefs will educate and inspire authentic Christian faith and practice in everyone who reads it but especially in the generations who will take the Wesleyan-holiness family into the future.

Discussion Questions

1. What do Maddix and Leclerc suggest about extreme positions of secular relativism and rigid religious absolutism?

2. What is the meaning of indoctrination? What is a Wesleyan response?

3. What is the meaning of truth from a Wesleyan perspective?

4. How do we discern between the essentials and nonessentials of our faith? Give examples.

5. In what ways are we to practice "catholic spirit," especially with other Christians who believe differently than we do?

Suggestions for Further Reading

Boone, Dan. *A Charitable Discourse: Talking About the Things That Divide Us.* Kansas City: Beacon Hill Press of Kansas City, 2010.

Lancaster, Sarah Heaner, Catherine Keller, Donald A. Thorsen, Dennis C. Dickerson, and Charles M. Wood. "What Makes Theology 'Wesleyan'?" *Methodist Review* 1 (2009).

Lodahl, Michael. *The Story of God: A Narrative Theology,* 2nd ed. Kansas City: Beacon Hill Press of Kansas City, 2008.

Maddix, Mark. "Understanding the Essentials." *Holiness Today.* Kansas City: Global Ministry Center, November/December 2011.

Maddox, Randy L. *Responsible Grace: John Wesley's Practical Theology.* Nashville: Kingswood, 1994.

PART 1
How to Do Theology

one
HOW AND WHY DO WE DO THEOLOGY?

Dick O. Eugenio

Theology is something we *do*. It is a noun, but it is also a verb. Thus, to theologize means to dig out Christian truth from a variety of sources (the most important source being Scripture) and to apply such truth to our present context. A really important question to ask, therefore, is: *As people belonging to the Wesleyan-holiness tradition, how should we* do *theology?* Is there a distinct Wesleyan procedure in theological reflection and formulation?

We must first address what we mean by theology and why we do theological thinking. These questions are essential because the term *theology* can sometimes be turned into something like a rotten tomato among church people when we even mention the word: It can instantly invite either raised eyebrows or snorts of derision, or both. Because some theologians have a penchant for technical jargon and complex explanations, theology as a field of study can become too professionalized and rather elitist, especially if it is done apart from the church! This separatism need not be the case, especially with Wesleyan theology.

Wesleyan theology looks first at Scripture's real-life circumstances as its source. Wesleyan theology is geared toward what Christians experience. Wesleyan theology is thoroughly practical. Wesleyan theology speaks and listens to its present-day context. And, finally, Wesleyan theology is all about love. None of these elements allow Wesleyan theology to be esoteric or irrelevant. All of them express a Wesleyan optimism.

Theology is simply *talk about God*, which every Christian does, intentionally or unintentionally. But different theologies, or theological traditions, have not only different doctrinal conclusions but also different ways of *doing* the theological task itself. Wesleyan theology is one tradition that has certain themes and doctrines that come out of a particular perspective about *how* we discover Christian truth.

Primary in our understanding is that theology should be focused on God's relationship with humanity. But how does theological discourse that is faithful to a relational understanding of God come about? This is not a new question. In fact, among Wesleyan scholars, there is no shortage of schematic paradigms that attempt to address the issue of how we *do* theology (sometimes called theological methodology).

One of the most important aspects of doing theology in a Wesleyan scheme is called *induction*, or inductive thinking. The Wesleyan approach is not an indoctrination of deductively learned conclusions but, rather, creative engagement and *inductive* thinking regarding real life situations and contexts that allow students of the Bible and of theology to engage the sources on deeper levels than simple memorization of facts. To be clear, deduction, or deductive thinking, is simply learning information that is already ordered and systematized. Induction involves exploration and discovery through relationships and through looking for the connections between Christian beliefs. *Conferencing* with others is the Wesleyan model of asking and responding to questions. It involves everyone in a worshiping community—leaders, scholars, theologians, and laypeople. All voices are heard with a spirit of humility. Wesleyan theological methodology draws individuals—in community and through relationships—to understand why we believe what we believe instead of just pushing them to acknowledge and commit to memory static Christian facts. Wesleyan theology lives and breathes and is dynamic and tenacious in its search for how beliefs apply to life today.

As Wesleyan theology is practiced, it is possible to see recurring themes, which we enumerate here as characteristic features of a chiefly Wesleyan mode of doing theological reflection. The proposals here are not original but represent a summary of an already prevalent way of thinking theologically in Wesleyan circles.

Our Foundation Is Scripture

The Wesleyan mode of theologizing, first and foremost, has Scripture as its authoritative foundation and source. Wesleyan theology is biblical—not in the microscopic sense of quoting Scripture to support a theological argument but—in the telescopic sense of looking at what the whole Bible might say about a particular theme. Thus, although theology engages culture, history, and other fields of study, these are not the primary interpretive tools in trying to make sense of Scripture; for Wesley, *Scripture* must interpret Scripture—which means that Wesleyan theologizing is rooted in the domain of biblical study more than in what is often called systematic theology or philosophical theology. Wesleyan theology looks at the primary source on its own bookshelf—the Bible (see chapter 2).

This reality does not imply, however, that sources other than Scripture are rejected outright. Wesleyans uphold the importance of the other three components of the quadrilateral—tradition, reason, and experience. Although they are not given equal authoritative status as Scripture, they are important in our theological discoveries and inductive style (see chapter 3). In the words of Steven L. Porter, "Wesleyan theological methodology upholds the supreme authority of Scripture, but maintains that the lesser lights of tradition, reason, and experience can aid in our understanding of Scripture."[1]

Our Orientation Is Experiential and Practical

Wesleyan theology values experience. Christian doctrine and practice are derived from Scripture, but they are also tested and confirmed by what we experience. As Kenneth Grider points out, Wesleyan theology is experiential because it is interested in our human situation and our religious-moral standing before God.[2] In the simplest way, theology, therefore, is the discourse about God's being and actions *in relation* to the created world from its beginning to its ultimate consummation. We not only believe in this relationship; we also *experience* it.

Theological thinking had long been using tradition and reason as aids, but Wesley's context brought experience to the forefront as another important instrument of understanding what rings theologically true. As such, again, Wesleyan theology is more focused on real life than just abstract thought. Wesley strongly believed that if a doctrine does not bear itself out experientially, it cannot be trusted. Moreover, in Wesleyan theology, experience is not merely a way to confirm theological truth; it is theology's very aim: Doctrine must *live*. A doctrine is formulated and taught in order for it to be experienced. But experience is also a source in the formulation itself. Therefore, Wesleyan theology is always relevant. It is not an enterprise geared toward intellectual amusement, but is always concerned with helping people undergo the experience it promotes.

If Wesleyan theology is experiential in orientation, it closely follows that Wesleyan theology is practical in application. Wesleyans have inherited John Wesley's *practical divinity*—where theology is primarily concerned with real life. Part of practical divinity is to take truth and apply it. For instance, in articulating who God is, Wesley was not concerned with God's *being* so much as with an active God whose being is always related to God's creative and redemptive actions toward the world. Instead of following the European philosophical and speculative theologizing procedure in the eighteenth and nineteenth centuries, Wesley theologized by applying theology to practical human and social needs.

---

1. Steven L. Porter, "Wesleyan Theological Methodology as a Theory of Integration," *Journal of Psychology and Theology* 32 (2004): 195.

2. J. Kenneth Grider, "The Nature of Wesleyan Theology," *Wesleyan Theological Journal* 17, no. 2 (1982): 43–57.

By nature, Wesleyan theology has an existential interest.[3] It does not engage in reflection without consideration of the practical situation of humanity and the world in relation to the holy God. Theology is neither predominantly propositional (concerned with concepts and statements) nor systematized (concerned with systematic arrangements of ideas). Faith is not intellectual assent to statements of truth; it is *trust* in God evidenced by love, obedience, worship, and the holy life. For this reason, Wesleyan theology is focused on salvation in outlook. We are interested in the question of how people might encounter the saving God in Jesus Christ and the Holy Spirit—from the prevenient work of grace to humanity's justification, sanctification, and growth in maturity. Ergo, Wesleyan theology is inescapably and intentionally *evangelical*. We are concerned with the salvation of sinful humanity and the persevering sanctification of the redeemed. (See chapters 12–15.)

Our Core Is Transformational Love

Wesleyan theology places holiness at its center, keeping in step with Wesley, for whom *holiness* was a key word.[4] Our doctrines of the triune God, salvation, sin, grace, church, and the last days are permeated with the distinct emphasis of our theological tradition—the doctrine and practice of holiness. Teaching and experiencing holiness of life are the ground and goal of Wesleyan theology—which means that, ultimately, Wesleyan theology is about love. The goal of theological teaching and reflection is that we might experience loving God with all our being, loving others as ourselves, and loving the created order in stewarding service. Our emphasis is the establishment of right relationships at both the vertical and horizontal levels.

Therefore, Wesleyan theology is primarily transformative. It has at its heart the goal to address humanity's needs for justification and sanctification. Wesley's theology possesses a deep-seated concern for the salvation of humanity.[5] The new birth, the new creation, and reconciliation to God are the basic objectives of our theological reflection, formulation, and proclamation. We theologize in order for people to be transformed into Christ's likeness.

Wesleyan theology is also transformational at the societal level.[6] Wesley himself was at the forefront of meeting the social needs of eighteenth-century England. This concern with society continued in the nineteenth and twentieth centu-

---

3. Ibid., 47–48.

4. Sarah Heaner Lancaster, Catherine Keller, Donald A. Thorsen, Dennis C. Dickerson, and Charles M. Wood, "What Makes Theology 'Wesleyan'?" *Methodist Review* 1 (2009): 16.

5. H. Ray Dunning, "Systematic Theology in a Wesleyan Mode," *Wesleyan Theological Journal* 17, no. 1 (1982): 17.

6. Lancaster et al., "What Makes Theology 'Wesleyan'?" 20–22.

ries as holiness denominations formed. Social involvement in Wesleyan theology is not an afterthought; rather, it is an essential at the very heart of our Wesleyan identity. We theologize, therefore, with both the individual person and greater society in mind. This duality makes Wesleyan theology inescapably holistic, for it seeks comprehensive salvation of the whole person and the whole world.

Our Outlook Is Optimistic

Wesleyan theology is realistic. It accepts the grim reality of sin. It is not blind to the distorted human situation and not oblivious to the comprehensive consequences of sin in the world. However, in the midst of this awareness is an optimism of grace. Wesleyans theologize with unashamed confidence in God's power to deal with the worst of human and cosmic predicaments. We engage in theological reflection with the redemptive and truly effective grace of God in mind. When we think about human and societal transformations, we embrace their possibility and actuality not in the light of human innate capacities but in the light of God's operative work in the world. It is for this reason that Wesleyan theology also has a strong doctrine of the Holy Spirit because we believe in the convicting, teaching, healing, and sanctifying work of God. This optimism even encompasses the future. Wesleyan theological reflection is characterized by a theology of hope.

Our Ethics Are Respons(e)-ible

Our confidence in God's grace does *not* imply the belief that redemption—both personal and cosmic—is realizable only through divine fiat, as if God does it all and we do nothing. Like our Calvinist brothers and sisters, we acknowledge God's rule, *but* Wesleyans also believe in God's empowering grace that makes humans both responsive and responsible. Grace works to enable human responsibility and action, not to override them.[7]

When thinking about salvation and transformation, Wesleyans consider the dynamic interaction between divine initiative, divine empowerment, and human responsibility.[8] This divine-human synergy, furthermore, is not only important at the initial stages of being born as children of God; it is also a continuous interaction between us and God that only ends in physical death. God's empowerment is neither merely occasional nor initiatory. It is uninterrupted until we are finally glorified in Jesus Christ. This means that the Christian life, from

---

7. Randy Maddox, *Responsible Grace: John Wesley's Practical Theology* (Nashville: Kingswood, 1994), 19.

8. This means that Wesleyan theologizing offers a via media between Protestant sola gratia and the Roman Catholic emphasis on holy works, thus taking the best of both traditions. George Croft Cell, *A Rediscovery of Wesley* (New York: H. Holt, 1935), 347.

beginning to end, is characterized by the dynamism of empowering grace and continuing human responsiveness and responsibility.

To conclude, we return to the question on how Wesleyans do theology. Wesleyans engage inductively in theological formulation by considering Scripture as the authoritative foundation while dialoguing with other sources and variables such as tradition, reason, and context. Wesleyans also theologize with a high regard for experience. Our concentration, therefore, is practice. We theologize not for the sake of theologizing but because we want to apply and experience God's work in our daily lives. As a result of our optimism about God's power and grace to enable humans to be responsible, our theology thinks of the best possible condition for human existence and our society—holiness in love and transformation. Overall, as God engages us and we respond to grace, our lives have meaning and purpose as we act as God's redemptive agents in the world.

Discussion Questions

1. How do we prepare Sunday school lessons and group studies in a way that is faithful to Wesleyan theology?

2. In an age of increasing relativism, how should we formulate and proclaim the message of holiness in a way that makes it compelling?

3. In what way is the Wesleyan theological method distinct from other theological traditions? How is it the same?

4. How can we as Wesleyans emphasize the practical and experiential without rejecting the intellectual and doctrinal aspects of our theology?

5. What are the dangers of emphasizing experience only in our theologizing?

Suggestions for Further Reading

Dunning, H. Ray. "Systematic Theology in a Wesleyan Mode." *Wesleyan Theological Journal* 17 (1982): 15–22.

Grider, J. Kenneth. *A Wesleyan-Holiness Theology*. Kansas City: Beacon Hill Press of Kansas City, 1994.

Lancaster, Sarah Heaner, Catherine Keller, Donald A. Thorsen, Dennis C. Dickerson, and Charles M. Wood. "What Makes Theology 'Wesleyan'?" *Methodist Review* 1 (2009): 7–26.

Maddox, Randy L. *Responsible Grace: John Wesley's Practical Theology*. Nashville: Kingswood, 1994.

McEwan, David B. *Wesley as a Practical Theologian: Theological Methodology in John Wesley's Doctrine of Christian Perfection.* Milton Keynes: Paternoster, 2011.

Porter, Steven L. "Wesleyan Theological Methodology as a Theory of Integration." *Journal of Psychology and Theology* 32 (2004): 190–99.

two

HOW DO WE READ THE BIBLE
FOR ALL IT IS WORTH?

———∞∞∞———

Celia I. Wolff

Wesleyans often claim "the primacy of Scripture" as a defining mark of their distinctive theological heritage.[1] In a 1739 letter Wesley maintains, "I allow no other rule, whether of faith or practice, than the Holy Scripture,"[2] but elsewhere he criticizes his lay preachers who claim, "I read only the Bible," by declaring, "This is rank enthusiasm. If you need no book but the Bible, you are got [sic] above St. Paul."[3]

---

1. See, for example, Randy L. Maddox, *Responsible Grace: John Wesley's Practical Theology* (Nashville: Abingdon Press, 1994), 36: "Given his correlation of definitive revelation with Scripture, it is no surprise that Wesley consistently identified the Bible as the most basic authority for determining Christian belief and practice."

Albert C. Outler, "The Wesleyan Quadrilateral in Wesley," *Wesleyan Theological Journal* 20, no. 1 (1985): 8: "When challenged for his authority, on any question, [Wesley's] first appeal was to the Holy Bible."

Donald A. D. Thorsen, "Interpretation in Interactive Balance: The Authority of Scripture for John Wesley," in *Reading the Bible in Wesleyan Ways: Some Constructive Proposals*, ed. Barry L. Callen and Richard P. Thompson (Kansas City: Beacon Hill Press of Kansas City, 2004), 81: "Perhaps John Wesley's most enduring contribution to theological method stems from his concern for catholicity in including experience along with Scripture, tradition, and reason as genuine sources of religious authority. While maintaining the primacy of Scripture, Wesley functioned with a dynamic interplay of sources in interpreting, illuminating, enriching, and communicating biblical truths."

2. John Wesley, *Letter to James Hervey*, March 20, 1739, accessed March 23, 2016, http://wesley.nnu/john-wesley-the-letters-of-john-wesley/wesley-letters-1739.

3. 1766 *Minutes*, Q. 30; also the "Large Minutes," Q. 32, *Works*, 8:315, quoted in Randy Maddox, "The Rule of Christian Faith, Practice, and Hope: John Wesley on the Bible," *Methodist Review* 3 no. 2 (2011): 1–35.

These quotations exemplify Wesley's contextual sensitivity whenever he made theological claims; he did not consider either declaration a rule for all times and places. More importantly, he cared more about Scripture's actual *function* in the life of the church than he did about haggling over complex issues about Scripture's authority. His practice reflects his claim that "Scripture should be the 'constant rule of all our tempers, all our words, and all our actions.'"[4] In this viewpoint Wesley implies that the best demonstration of Scripture's authority is its lived interpretation.

At the same time, Wesley's own practice (as well as his explicit warnings above) shows the need for good guides and mentors. Good biblical interpretation must energize good *lived* interpretation. To read the Bible as a Wesleyan is to regard John Wesley as a mentor. If "the appropriate relationship to one's mentors is openness both to embracing the wisdom that they offer and to discerning the contexuality and limitations of their example," then a Wesleyan attitude to the Bible need not agree with Wesley in every detail but will evaluate his overall aims and strategy in light of their applicability today.[5] Wesley read the Bible as the primary guide for Christian faith, practice, and hope; he read and encouraged others to read the Bible in order to live a Scripture-shaped life.[6]

Wesleyans today may largely read the Bible for the same purposes as Wesley, and so may also fruitfully adopt many of his reading practices. Whether consciously or otherwise, Wesley chose reading *practices* for their usefulness toward his *purpose*, always in light of the *context* in which he and his congregations lived and ministered. Wesley's contextual sensitivity guided his practical decisions about reading Scripture. Exactly by emulating Wesley's eye for the power of practices toward a purpose in context, Wesleyans today might adopt new, additional, altered, or other practices than Wesley chose in order to pursue a Scripture-shaped life in today's world. Five reading practices for today are outlined here—derived directly from Wesley and from emulating his embrace of a wide span of Christian tradition.

1. Read. The whole Bible. Regularly.

The most basic Wesleyan habit of reading the Bible is immersion. Nothing replaces *frequent* reading of the whole Bible. Wesley encouraged all Methodists to saturate their minds and hearts with Scripture for two hours daily[7]—not just favorite passages, but all of the Bible[8]—in the hope of shaping even the language

---

4. Maddox, *Responsible Grace*, 37.

5. Maddox, "Rule of Christian Faith." This essay relies heavily on Maddox's evaluation of John Wesley's claims and habits regarding Scripture.

6. Ibid., 30–34.

7. Ibid., 33.

8. Ibid., 16.

they used in daily life.[9] While most church folk in the modern world will not find such a practice feasible, Wesley's exhortation conveys four key ideas:

- Reading the Bible is for everyone; no one need be intimidated out of reading the Bible.
- No one can read the Bible for someone else.
- No one can read the Bible too much.
- No one can read too much of the Bible.

But reading at all is only the beginning. The devil quoting from the Old Testament in Jesus's temptation story demonstrates that knowledge of the Bible's words does not always result in sound interpretation (Matt. 4:1–11; Luke 4:1–13). So the *how* of reading matters too.

2. Read to the best of your ability.

Reading the Bible resembles other arts, crafts, and sports in which some people engage professionally but in which one need not be an expert to find the activity enjoyable or edifying. The most important tools for reading the Bible require no special expertise:

- **Pay attention to words.** Good readers of the Bible meld a grandparent's patient perseverance with a toddler's relentless curiosity; they examine each word, fearlessly ask questions, and investigate every hidden corner of the text—because every word matters.
- **Use language resources.** Without knowledge of Hebrew and Greek, English speakers would do best to begin with a translation that maintains transparency to the original languages,[10] but many modern resources—interlinear Bibles, lexicons, concordances, online Bible resources, etc.—allow readers without original language facility to study the words of Scripture at a depth laypeople in Wesley's day could not approach.[11]

---

9. Ibid., 32.

10. When people ask me which translation I prefer, I recommend some combination of the Revised Standard Version and the New Revised Standard Version. While I don't always care for the antiquated language of the RSV, I prefer it overall because of its general transparency to the original languages. Of course, no translation is perfect or completely adequate; those who cannot study the original languages should compare several translations and/or use the resources outlined below.

11. For a good New Testament interlinear, I recommend the *New Greek-English Interlinear New Testament,* trans. R. K. Brown and P. W. Comfort, ed. J. D. Douglas (Carol Stream, IL: Tyndale, 1990).

I recommend using this interlinear in concert with the *Greek-English Concordance New Testament,* ed. J.R. Kohlenberger III et al, (Grand Rapids: Zondervan, 1997).

Kohlenberger also has the *NIV Interlinear Hebrew-English Old Testament* (Grand Rapids: Zondervan, 1993), which can be fruitfully used alongside his *Hebrew-English Concordance to the Old Testament* (Grand Rapids: Zondervan, 1998).

- **Note key features of the literature.** The Bible contains many genres—various kinds of narrative, law codes, poetry, letters, even a sermon or two. A good reader asks, *What kind of document am I reading?* A good reader also treats each document as a *whole.* Each book of the Bible is a whole literary document meant to be read in its entirety and integrity.
- **Study the context.** Each book of the Bible originated in a time and place very different from twenty-first-century Western culture. These cultures and contexts merit their own study because language makes sense only in context. Sometimes a book will tell enough about the context for a reasonably sensitive reading, but if such markers are lacking, a study Bible introduction or a Bible dictionary article can quickly provide a reader with helpful information.[12]

3. Read with others in a spirit of humility.

C. S. Lewis summarizes aptly the principles on which Wesley commends reading the Bible with many and various others: "What you see and hear depends a good deal on where you are standing: it also depends on what sort of person you are."[13] Reading with others expands a person's experiential perspective as well as shapes character by exposing that person to exemplary lived interpretation. Allowing others to influence one's perspective demands the humility to recognize one's limitations—as Wesley did.[14] Such humility also opens a person to receiving the Holy Spirit's guidance through others. Which others?

Many free resources are also available online: Bible Gateway (www.biblegateway.com) offers many translations searchable by word, phrase, or passage. It is a great place to begin studying particular words, but for real accuracy, one needs original language access.

All the free, original-language online resources I know rely on outdated scholarship. Many are coded to Strong's concordance numbers, which prove useful even if they are outdated. BibleStudyTools has a searchable interlinear, including both Testaments (www.biblestudy tools.com/interlinear-bible) as well as many other resources; BibleGT (greattreasures.org) allows for in-depth analysis of the New Testament.

With free online resources, it is important to keep in mind that you get what you pay for. For biblical study that uses the best available scholarship, it is best to plan a trip to a theological/academic library or spend a little money procuring a few key resources.

12. The *HarperCollins Study Bible*, *Access Bible*, and the *New Oxford Annotated Bible* are all good resources. Bible dictionaries come in both single- and multivolume versions. The *HarperCollins Bible Dictionary* is a good single volume for beginning students. The *New Interpreter's Dictionary of the Bible* is five volumes and geared toward intermediate students. The *Anchor Bible Dictionary* is fourteen volumes and written for more advanced students. For a free resource, the website www.bibleodyssey.com is exceptionally good—accessible writing, useful information, and cutting-edge scholarship.

13. C. S. Lewis, *The Magician's Nephew* (New York: Macmillan Publishing Company, 1955), 125.

14. Maddox, "Rule of Christian Faith," 18.

- **Christian tradition and the rule of faith.** Wesley drew from a wide range of Christian tradition, and especially from Christian writers in the first three centuries of the church's life.[15] He privileged what early Christian theologians call the "rule of faith," summarized in the traditional Christian creeds.[16] These guides fence the field of scriptural interpretation. Embracing the rule of faith helps Christians stay honest about our basic theological convictions and guard against spurious pretentions to certainty about matters of faith.[17]

- **Saints and advanced disciples.** Since Wesley's purpose in reading the Bible was to form a Scripture-shaped life, he commended learning from those who have long traveled the road of discipleship and lead exemplary lives.[18] People who live and love like Jesus have special insight into Scripture; their very lives illuminate the text. Wesley privileged the Christian tradition and advanced disciples, but he also sought dialogue expressly with those who did not share his viewpoints.[19] This habit might lead today's Wesleyans to engage beyond boundaries Wesley himself did not explicitly commend or practice.

- **Marginalized and underprivileged people.** The focus of Jesus's ministry suggests that socially marginalized people have ears especially tuned to how the reign of God is good news. For social elites, the gospel's leveling of worldly power may not sound like good news. Hearing the gospel among the oppressed reminds the privileged of God's universal care and the goodness of that message. So modern readers must seek those who have different perspectives, who differ according to culturally defined status markers—for example, those who differ from oneself in gender, race, ethnicity, national origin, economic class, and the like.

- **People of other faith traditions or no faith.** Reading with those who do not share Christians' basic understanding of God and reality keeps us honest about what we take away from Scripture and the reasons for our belief. They recall to our attention the questions we still struggle to answer as well as the portions of the Bible that make us uncomfortable,

---

15. Ibid., 19–21.

16. Ibid., 21–24.

17. The *Ancient Christian Commentary on Scripture* (ed. Thomas C. Oden, InterVarsity Press) has single-volume collections of early Christian writings for each book of the Bible. Eerdmans Publishing Company is in the process of publishing a similar but more comprehensive series titled *The Church's Bible*. The Christian Classics Ethereal Library aggregates much of the relevant material, the translations of which are in the public domain, including the multi-volume series edited by Phillip Schaff, *Ante-Nicene Fathers* and *Nicene and Post-Nicene Fathers* (www.ccel.org).

18. Maddox, "Rule of Christian Faith," 18.

19. Ibid., 19.

and so can drive us to read more, and more deeply. Reading with such others in a spirit of humility and welcome belongs properly to Christian hospitality and witness, and safeguards against making Scripture a mere mirror of personal biases.

4. Read through a lens of God's universal offer of mercy.

If Wesley had a favorite verse of Scripture, among the top candidates would be Psalm 145:9: "The LORD is good to all: and his tender mercies are over all his works" (KJV).[20] Wesley understood the Bible as God's written teaching on the one thing he most wanted to know—"the way to heaven."[21] Reading the Bible through the lens of God's infinite compassion realizes the possibility of salvation for all. This lens led Wesley to shun any reading of biblical passages that would exclude anyone from God's saving care. Modern Wesleyans may conceive salvation more broadly than "the way to heaven," but viewing the whole Bible through passages that highlight God's active love for all of creation remains a sound Wesleyan interpretive lens.

5. Read the Bible as a story.

The Bible's length and the diversity of texts within it can obscure the fact that it has a narrative arc. The narrative arc is subtler than in a conventional novel, but as in a novel—even one as long and complex as *The Brothers Karamazov* or *War and Peace*—a good reader remembers the narrative context of each episode. Many interpreters of Christian Scripture have noticed the Bible's overall narrative arc and have proposed further ways of dividing up the story. Dividing the story helps the reader both to remember that the whole Bible *is* a story and to maintain a frame of reference *within* the story. One such model conceives the story as a five-act drama consisting of Creation, Covenant, Christ, Church, and Consummation.[22] These divisions emphasize God's merciful work on behalf of creation—from beginning to end.

Wesley recognized the Bible's coherence in tenor and scope, and understood well the importance of reading with a sense of literary context, but he did not place any particular emphasis on the Bible's narrative coherence. Yet, a sense of the story that bends toward highlighting God's constant generosity can, even so, properly bear the name *Wesleyan*, especially if it helps readers of the Bible live Scripture-shaped lives.

---

20. Ibid., 26–30.

21. Ibid., 2 n. 1.

22. The five-act drama model comes from Samuel Wells, *Improvisation: The Drama of Christian Ethics* (Grand Rapids: Brazos Press, 2004), especially chapters 3–4.

Improvising a Scripture-Shaped Life

The above outline of the Bible's story helps define the shape of a Scripture-shaped life.[23] This five-act drama shows the key moments of God's action that give the story its overall character, and makes room on the stage, so to speak, for the church's ongoing life between Christ and Consummation. Within this dramatic narrative space, Christians improvise based on the two acts that frame the church's life. Because the focal point of the whole story is the figure of Jesus, Christians particularly aim to emulate Jesus's lived interpretation of the Old Testament. Through trusting that God has already arranged how the story will end, Christians can focus on faithfulness to Jesus and his way of life rather than worrying about the story's outcome. Such ways of thinking about a Scripture-shaped life can help the church to recognize its freedom to play and practice within the boundaries of God's story—not just as readers of the Bible but also as a community that visibly lives its interpretation of Scripture in a world that is hungry for life, truth, and love.

Discussion Questions

1. Which portions of the Bible have you most focused on in your own reading? What are some areas of the Bible you might fruitfully engage more frequently?

2. What reading practices outlined under the heading *Read to the best of your ability* have you used before? Which are new to you? What practices have proven most enriching for you?

3. Who are some of the saints and mature disciples who influence your thought about God? In what ways might they inform your reading of the Bible?

4. What do you understand by the phrase *a Scripture-shaped life*? What might be some of the key features of such a life?

Suggestions for Further Reading

Callen, Barry L. and Richard P. Thompson, eds. *Reading the Bible in Wesleyan Ways: Some Constructive Proposals.* Kansas City: Beacon Hill Press of Kansas City, 2004.

Davis, Ellen F. and Richard B. Hays. "Nine Theses on the Art of Reading Scripture." In *The Art of Reading Scripture*, edited by Davis and Hays, 1-5. Grand Rapids: Eerdmans, 2002.

23. This conclusion more or less summarizes key points from chapters 3–4 of Wells, *Improvisation.*

Ekblad, Bob. *Reading the Bible with the Damned.* Louisville: Westminster John Knox Press, 2005.

Hays, Richard. "Exegesis." In *Concise Encyclopedia of Preaching*, edited by William H. Willimon and Richard Lischer, 122–28. Louisville: Westminster John Knox Press, 1995.

Maddox, Randy. "The Rule of Christian Faith, Practice, and Hope: John Wesley on the Bible." *Methodist Review* 3, no. 2 (2011): 1–35.

Wells, Samuel. *Improvisation: The Drama of Christian Ethics.* Grand Rapids: Brazos Press, 2004.

three
WHAT IS THE WESLEYAN QUADRILATERAL?

———— ✺✺✺ ————

John Grant

For John Wesley, Scripture was the preeminent—indeed, the primary—source for religious truth. Scripture alone stood as the complete rule of faith and practice, clearly pointing out the way of salvation. But Wesley also understood that at times Scripture needs to be explained in order to be clear. He believed in the primacy of Scripture, offered specific advice on how to view it and how to use it, and did not assume it would always read clearly. Scripture often needs to be interpreted; sometimes a certain passage needs to be understood in light of the whole. At times, one must visit many other verses in order to interpret a specific passage. But at other times, sources outside Scripture itself also need to be used. Wesley would never place one of these sources above Scripture. But he did affirm that tradition, reason, and experience can aid in understanding what Scripture means and how it is to be applied to the present situation. Scholars have coined the phrase *the Wesleyan quadrilateral* to refer to this set of four. Scripture always sings the lead, but the other three harmonize so the melody can ring even more true.

Tradition

To achieve a harmonious truth, Wesley often placed tradition next to Scripture in a supporting role. In a letter to a Dr. Middleton, Wesley defended his use of tradition in this way:

> The Scriptures are a complete rule of faith and practice; and they are clear in all necessary points. And yet their clearness does not prove that they need not be explained, nor their completeness that they need not be enforced. The esteeming the writings of the first three centuries not equally with but next

36

to the Scriptures never carried any man yet into dangerous errors, nor probably ever will. But it has brought many out of dangerous errors.[1]

Tradition for Wesley, however, should not be understood in too broad a sense that would include the whole sweep of Christian history from the early church to the present age. Wesley was selective. Tradition only had authority when it embodied the consensus of Christian teaching and practice, thus exhibiting continuity with the apostolic church.[2] His interest in and appeal to tradition were rooted in his understanding of what he considered to be religion in its purest form. And Wesley found this sort of purity in the writings from the early church (primarily the first three centuries) and in the standard doctrines of the Anglican church as affirmed in the Anglican Articles, Homilies, and the Book of Common Prayer.[3]

Additionally, Wesley's selectiveness in appealing to tradition should also be attributed to Wesley's *soteriological* focus—that is, his interest in the doctrine of salvation. (See chapter 12.) Donald Thorsen points out that, for Wesley, the appeal to tradition was not simply *ecclesial*, in that it sought to establish some sort of unbroken ecclesiastical succession from the ancient church to the church of his day, but that it was instead focused on the understanding of a salvation that fundamentally consisted of justification by faith and the accompanying commitment to a life of holy living.[4] In this sense, Wesley's appeal to and use of tradition went deeper than simply doctrinal or church issues; it was essentially *spiritual*.[5]

Wesley's use of tradition to explain and enforce Scripture's meaning had a practical aspect to it—or, as Ted Campbell puts it, it was "programmatic." In other words, Wesley saw in the writings and in the lives of the saints of the early church a model for contemporary Christians. In their faith, virtue, and holiness Wesley found support for what he saw as the distinctive teachings and practices of the people called Methodist.[6] This is not to say that Wesley idolized the past. His was not, as Randy Maddox put it, a "totally naïve primitivism."[7] He recognized there were problems and errors. The past was not infallible. He sought his way through the problems and errors of tradition with the help of Scripture's guidance and the proper use of reason.

---

1. Wesley, "A Letter to The Reverend Dr. Conyers Middleton," in *Works*, [*Works*, 10:14.]

2. Ted A. Campbell, "The Interpretive Role of Tradition," in *Wesley and the Quadrilateral: Renewing the Conversation*, W. Stephen Gunter et al. (Nashville: Abingdon Press, 1997), 69.

3. Maddox, *Responsible Grace*, 42.

4. Donald A. D. Thorsen, *The Wesleyan Quadrilateral: Scripture, Tradition, Reason and Experience as a Model of Evangelical Theology* (Grand Rapids: Zondervan, 1990), 163–64.

5. Ibid., 152.

6. Campbell, "Interpretive Role of Tradition," 72.

7. Maddox, *Responsible Grace*, 43.

Reason

Randy Maddox points out that next to Scripture, Wesley appealed to reason most often in defending authentic Christianity. As a matter of fact, Wesley referred to Scripture and reason together more often than he did to Scripture alone.[8] Wesley had a high regard for reason and for reason's role in religion. In a letter to Dr. Rutherforth written in March 1768, Wesley claims, "It is a fundamental principle with us, that to renounce reason is to renounce religion; that religion and reason go hand in hand; and that all irrational religion is false religion."[9] As with his use of tradition, however, we need to understand what Wesley meant by reason and what the limits of reason are.

Undoubtedly, the cultural milieu of the early Enlightenment period had an influence on Wesley's understanding of reason. After all, it was the "Age of Reason." And, both within the Anglican church of his day and throughout the general population of England, there was a growing confidence in the power of reason. Wesley shared this confidence. But it was a confidence bound to a specific understanding and use of reason.

Wesley rejected the idea held by many of the rationalists of his day that knowledge was something innate, a truth within, something embedded within all human beings from birth. For the rationalist, reason was an independent source of knowledge. Reason was used to discover a truth that was already there. Contrary to this understanding of reason, Wesley held that reason was not an independent source of knowledge but was, instead, only a processor. Along with the empiricists of his day, Wesley held that knowledge comes from our experiences through the five senses. It is external to us. In a sermon on Hebrews 11:1, Wesley insists that, "All the knowledge which we naturally have is originally derived from our senses."[10] This made reason a sort of tool for processing the data that our senses take in, which includes the revelation of Scripture and of God within nature.[11]

Despite the great importance Wesley placed on reason, there were limits. As Rebekah Miles puts it, "Reason alone can accomplish very little; reason in good company can do many things."[12] Reason alone cannot produce faith. And while reason reflecting on creation may lead us to know that God exists, it cannot cause us to know God, or what God's character is like. For that, more is needed. And, perhaps most importantly, reason cannot produce the sort of virtue that

---

8. Ibid., 40.

9. Wesley, "Letter to Dr. Rutherforth," in *Works*, 14:354.

10. Wesley, "On the Discovery of Faith," in *Works*, 7:231.

11. For more, see Rebekah Miles, "Instrumental Role of Reason," in *Wesley and the Quadrilateral*, 84–86.

12. Ibid., 94.

leads to a life of love, holiness, and genuine happiness. As Wesley puts it in his sermon "The Case of Reason Considered":

> Let reason do all that reason can; Employ it as far as it will go. But, at the same time, acknowledge it is utterly incapable of giving either faith, or hope, or love; and, consequently, of producing either real virtue, or substantial happiness. Expect these from a higher source, even from the Father of the spirits of all flesh.[13]

Experience

To the two subordinating authorities of tradition and reason, Wesley added experience. Albert Outler notes, "It was Wesley's special genius that he conceived of adding 'experience' to the traditional Anglican triad, and thereby adding vitality without altering the substance."[14] Wesley wanted to guard against a form of religion that was purely rationalistic. His insistence on a "heart religion" was meant to move religion from a dead, theoretical faith to a vital, existential one.[15] His fear was not that "the people called Methodists should ever cease to exist" but that they would exist as a "dead sect, having the form of religion without the power."[16] In order for religion to be meaningful, it must be vital. Correct doctrine that is not lived out in the experiences of the believer is a dead doctrine.

This vital experience of God in the life of the believer became important for understanding Wesley's ideas regarding both conversion and the assurance of the Spirit. For Wesley, these were the two primary ways in which a person was able to experience a *direct* awareness of God. As Wesley puts it: "The testimony of the Spirit is an inward impression on the soul, whereby the Spirit of God directly witnesses to my spirit, that I am a child of God; that Jesus Christ hath loved me, and given himself for me; and that all my sins are blotted out, and I, even I, am reconciled to God."[17] This direct awareness was so important for Wesley that, in a second sermon on the witness of the Spirit, he insists that a believer "cannot be satisfied with any thing less than a direct testimony from his Spirit, that he is 'merciful to their unrighteousness, and remembers their sins and iniquities no more.'"[18]

Experience was also used to confirm or test proposed interpretations of Scripture. Wesley believed that the truths of Scripture are confirmed by experience. If a particular piece of Scripture seems to be saying one thing but there is

---

13. Wesley, "The Case of Reason Considered," in *Works*, 6:360.
14. Albert Cook Outler, "The Wesleyan Quadrilateral in John Wesley," *Wesleyan Theological Journal* 20, no. 1 (1985): 10.
15. Ibid.
16. Wesley, "Thoughts upon Methodism," in *Works*, 13:258.
17. Wesley, "The Witness of the Spirit," in *Works*, 5:115.
18. Wesley, "The Witness of the Spirit: Discourse II," in *Works*, 5:128.

little or no evidence of that actually being lived out in the lives of believers, Wesley believed that he must then reconsider his interpretation. Besides confirming the truth of Scripture, experience could give insight into forming doctrines and practices that do not seem to be mentioned in Scripture, places where Scripture is silent. Perhaps this is most clearly seen in the debate over entire sanctification, whether God works it gradually or instantaneously.

Believing Scripture to be silent on this particular topic, Wesley looked for an answer in the experiences of the lives of Christians across time, and in the lives of his Methodists. His opinion was shaped by the survey of the experiences of numerous Christians. Interestingly, that opinion changed over time. In this way Wesley believed we can go beyond Scripture but never against Scripture.[19]

In looking at how John Wesley used tradition, reason, and experience in a supporting role alongside Scripture, we can appreciate how he looked for a balanced middle road. Though in and of themselves they were not sources of truth *per se*, tradition, reason, and experience did help bring light and add vitality to the truth of Scripture. Additionally, besides using tradition, reason, and experience to test and enforce the reasonableness of particular doctrines (particularly those distinct to Methodists), Wesley had a practical application of their use. For Wesley, the goal was to live out a life of love to God and neighbor. Tradition, reason, and experience help to form the practices and doctrines that produce a Christlike character, promote holiness, and stir the heart to love. It is perhaps this practical and vital aspect that, in the end, is the most important.

Discussion Questions

1. How do Wesley's claims that "to renounce reason is to renounce religion" and that "all irrational religion is false religion" make you feel? How is Wesley right or wrong?

2. Wesley understood reason as a tool. By itself it could do little. How do you see Scripture and faith functioning alongside reason?

3. Do you think Wesley's addition of experience is beneficial, or do you see it causing more problems than it settles (the problems of purely subjective feelings, for example)? How might we avoid these problems?

4. Is it essential that all believers have the assurance of salvation Wesley spoke of? How can we account for differences in experience? Does there have to be a norm about how we experience God?

---

19. Maddox, *Responsible Grace*, 46, 43.

Suggestions for Further Reading

Gunter, Stephen W., et al. *Wesley and the Quadrilateral: Renewing the Conversation.* Nashville: Abingdon Press, 1997.

Maddox, Randy, L. *Responsible Grace: John Wesley's Practical Theology.* Nashville: Kingswood, 1994.

Thorsen, Donald A. D. *The Wesleyan Quadrilateral: Scripture, Tradition, Reason and Experience as a Model of Evangelical Theology.* Grand Rapids: Zondervan, 1990.

Wesley, John. "The Witness of the Spirit." Discourse I and II. Vol. 5 of *The Works of John Wesley,* edited by Thomas Jackson. Kansas City: Beacon Hill Press of Kansas City, 1978.

———. "Earnest Appeal to Men of Reason and Religion" and "A Farther Appeal to Men of Reason and Religion." Vol. 8 of *The Works of John Wesley.*

PART 2
Who God Is

four
HOW CAN WE UNDERSTAND THE TRINITY?

———— ᢒᢒᢒ ————

Timothy R. Gaines

Let's say it up front: The doctrine of the Trinity is complex. Centuries of work by the church's most accomplished scholars have come to agree upon this much: *The Trinity is a mystery.* What, then, is the worth of such a doctrine for Christian life and practice? Isn't the doctrine of the Trinity a mystery beyond our comprehension, a metaphysical riddle offered up for the banter of philosophers and theologians? Does it really bear any significance for daily Christian life?

When treated primarily as a set of ideas and propositions about God, the importance of the doctrine of the Trinity for daily Christian life often becomes difficult to ascertain. If, however, the doctrine of the Trinity assumes a role of describing the ways in which we are being drawn into God's love and redemption, its importance for daily life will be difficult to contain. Because the Wesleyan tradition often tends to do theology with a keen eye toward what doctrine means for our salvation, our approach to the Trinity is one that is not as concerned with unlocking the mysterious "manner how"[1] of God's life for the sake of gaining information as much as it is to become caught up in the love of the Father, Son, and Holy Spirit, that we might know God's redemption in full, complete, and comprehensive ways, ultimately leaving us "lost in wonder, love and praise."[2]

This is not to say that we ought to give up all attempts at describing God. Rather, we are like the one who has encountered the majesty of a mountaintop sunset but whose attempt to describe what she or he saw, vivid as it may be, fails to capture the fullness of the spectacle. We speak of the Trinity not because we can comprehensively explain God but because we do not want to be reduced to silence after encountering such goodness.

---

1. Wesley, "On the Trinity," in *Works,* 6:204.
2. Charles Wesley, "Love Divine, All Loves Excelling," in *Worship in Song: Hymnal* (Kansas City: Lillenas Publishing Co., 1972), 16.

How, then, do we speak of Trinity? Generally, Trinitarian theology proceeds by giving special attention to: (1) who God *is* as Trinity and (2) what God *does* as Trinity.[3]

Substantially Love, In Mystical Three: Who God Is as Trinity

Historically, the questions related to who God is as Trinity have dealt with how God can be three-in-one without being different gods, how each Person (a carefully chosen word, not to be mistaken with human) of the Trinity is divine, and how each Person relates to the other two. When done well, this has been a task of describing what God has revealed to us, rather than prescribing how we think God ought to be. God's self-revelation in the sending of the Son and the Holy Spirit are the starting places from which the church attempts to describe the redemptive reality of God-with-us.

After centuries of Spirit-led deliberation, the description upon which the church has largely agreed is that God *is* Father, Son, and Holy Spirit; these three subsist in inseparable unity; each is fully the divine being; this is the one God.[4] This terminology, represented by Figure 1, stands opposed to a common (mis)interpretation of the Trinity, represented in Figure 2:

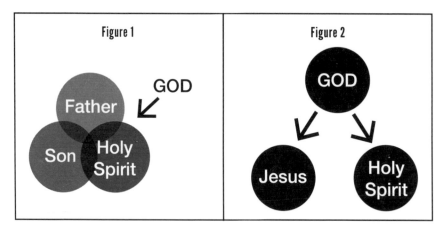

The approach illustrated in Figure 2 often conflates God into Father, leading to a fair amount of theological confusion over what we are to do with the Son and the Holy Spirit. While Figure 2 starts by easily maintaining the unity of God, problems immediately arise when we attempt to make sense of who Jesus

---

3. Theologians often use the term *essential Trinity* to denote questions about who God *is* as Trinity and the term *economic Trinity* to refer to what God *does* as Trinity.

4. See Samuel M. Powell, *Discovering Our Christian Faith: An Introduction to Christian Theology* (Kansas City: Beacon Hill Press of Kansas City, 2008).

and the Holy Spirit are in relation to God. If the Son and the Spirit are not essentially God, don't we have three gods? And if the Son and the Spirit are essentially God, how is God one (Deut. 6:4)?

Figure 1, on the other hand, reflects the confession that the one God is a relational communion of the Father, Son, and Holy Spirit and that these three together are one God. While there is inseparable unity among the Father, Son, and Holy Spirit (John 17:21), there is also relationality; each Person of the Trinity relates to the others in the inseparable unity of perfect love.

If we would say anything about who God is as Trinity, it is this: God *is* love (1 John 4:8). There is no relation of the Father, Son, and Holy Spirit that is not characterized as love. In the essence of who God is as a communion of holy love, the Father, Son, and Holy Spirit do not disappear into one another, conflating into a single, relationless totality. Rather, the unity of who God is as love comes precisely as the Father, Son, and Spirit are inseparably united in their love for one another. This is how, as Charles Wesley has so wonderfully hymned, God is "substantially love, in mystical three,"[5] "pure essential love" as Father, Son, and Holy Spirit.[6]

Understanding God as a single communion of three divine persons stretches our theological imaginations and reminds us that, though we are made in God's image, God is not made in ours. As a triune being, God's life, to say it simply, is *different* from ours. Categories like gender are difficult—impossible, even—to apply to God. The question, *Is God male or female?* is best answered, *God is triune.* While the Word became flesh as a male, we would be hard-pressed to ascribe maleness back onto the fullness of God's triune being. Scripture obviously uses the masculine descriptors of Father and Son; these are used in this chapter. But the relationship between the Father and Son is characterized by self-giving, rather than any stereotypically masculine images of power and domination. God's life as Trinity is the image in which humans have been created, and that image is essentially self-giving love.

Lead Our Hearts into His Love: What God Does as Trinity

If love is the essence of who God is, what might that mean for what God does as Trinity? The doctrine of the Trinity is our good-faith attempt to describe what God has revealed to us. We must keep in mind, however, that the way God has revealed God's self to us is by giving God's self to us and for us, exemplified most fully by the Son on the cross (Phil. 2:7). Saying, "Father, Son, and Holy Spirit," then, is not only descriptive of who God *is*, but it is simultaneously

---

5. Charles Wesley, "Hymn XXIII," in *Trinity Hymns (1767)*, ed. Randy Maddox (Durham: Duke Center for Studies in the Wesleyan Tradition, 2008), 106.

6. Charles Wesley, "Hymn XIV," in ibid., 98.

descriptive of what God *does*—a telling of the narrative of God's salvation in a truncated way.[7] How has God acted to save us? Through the Father sending the Son in the power of the Spirit.

The very self-giving of God that allows us to glimpse who God *is* as Trinity is the sending of the Son and the Spirit for our salvation—or, what God *does* as Trinity. Every bit of God's self-giving is also God's self-revelation; God has not acted to redeem as an idea or proposition but as being personally present with creation, enfolding it within the perfect love of the Trinity. "Thy love, thyself" is how Charles Wesley sang of this union, so that where God's love is, there is God.[8] Therefore, the sending of the Son and the Spirit are far more than a divine deposit into creation; they are the gracious acts of God's very life being opened to us and a simultaneous invitation to live *within* the redemptive love of the Father, Son, and Holy Spirit.

John's gospel gives us a poignantly vivid depiction of the reality of the Trinity. After his resurrection, Jesus appears to his disciples, his body still marked by the wounds of his crucifixion. "Put your finger here," Jesus says to Thomas. "Reach out your hand and put it into my side" (John 20:27). Jesus's side, and the wound he is inviting Thomas to enter, is the very place from which the fluids of life drained from Jesus's body, where his life was literally broken open (John 19:34). We might say that in the sending of the Son, the life of God as Trinity is broken open to us, and the place where God's life is broken open is now the point of entry, complete with an invitation to enter into perfect love and be redeemed by that love.

The doctrine of the Trinity tells us that our God is the one who has chosen to be broken open for our sake, not only to give us love but also to give us a place in the love that constitutes the relationships of the Father, Son, and Holy Spirit. Rather than being a clever solution to an unsolvable idea, then, the doctrine of the Trinity is the description of the way God has acted so that we can be caught up in the redemptive flow of love divine.

The love that flows out from God in the sending of the Son and the Spirit is the love that also draws us into the flow of God's love, that we might be *renewed*. One of the distinctly Wesleyan views of what takes place in God's redemption is that we humans are "renewed in love,"[9] a love "excluding sin, filling the heart, taking up the whole capacity of the soul."[10] For Wesley, this love was a gift given only by God. As we are drawn into the redemptive love of God, Wesley taught,

---

7. See Robert Jenson, *Systematic Theology* (Oxford: Oxford University Press, 1997), 1:46.

8. Charles Wesley, "Hymn XXX," in *Trinity Hymns*, 114.

9. John Wesley, *A Plain Account of Christian Perfection* (Kansas City: Beacon Hill Press of Kansas City, 1966), 91 ff.

10. John Wesley, "The Scripture Way of Salvation," in *John Wesley's Sermons: An Anthology*, ed. Albert C. Outler and Richard P. Heitzenrater (Nashville: Abingdon Press, 1991), 374.

we are renewed by love in God's image, that we might live into God's original intent for humanity, that humans be "what God is, Love"[11] (see chapter 8). This is not to say that humans become divine in the way that God is divine, but it is to say that as we plunge deeply into the love that *is* God, that love *does* something: It renews us, that we might embody the image of God. Of course, all of this is a work done by God; God not only self-gives and self-reveals, but that same self-giving is precisely what makes participating in God's love possible. We are gathered into the life of God's love to the glory of the Father, through the Son, in the power of the Spirit. "Come, Holy Ghost," was Charles Wesley's lyrical prayer, "and lead our hearts *into* his love."[12]

Thy Love, Thyself, And Lo! I Live

"The knowledge of the Three-One God," John Wesley writes, "is interwoven with all true Christian faith; with all vital religion."[13] That knowledge, however, is not knowledge that comes propositionally. It is the knowledge that can only come from being in the love that is God's three-one life. The doctrine of the Trinity is essential for Christian life and practice precisely because being in the love of the Father, Son, and Holy Spirit is the way in which we are redeemed, restored, and renewed in God's image. The doctrine of the Trinity is not only helpful for Christian life and practice; it is the very content of our salvation! Having been so graced, we do well to join in Charles Wesley's hymnic prayer:

O wouldst thou stamp it now on mine [heart]
The name and character divine
The holy One in Three!
Come, Father, Son and Spirit, give
Thy love, —thyself: and lo! I live
Imparadis'd in thee.[14]

Discussion Questions

1. How do you think our ideas about the Trinity change when we focus more on the Trinity as the way in which God acts to save us, rather than as a set of ideas about God?

2. What do you think the doctrine of the Trinity suggests to us about the relationship between who God is and what God does?

11. Wesley, "The Image of God," in ibid., 15.
12. Charles Wesley, "Hymn CVI," in *Trinity Hymns*, 68. Emphasis added.
13. John Wesley, "On the Trinity," *Works* 6:205.
14. Charles Wesley, "Hymn XXX," 114.

3. What implications do you see in making the distinction between God giving us love and God giving us a place *in* the love of the Father, Son, and Holy Spirit?

4. If the doctrine of the Trinity tells us, in part, about how God is broken open to us, what do you think that says about the nature of God?

Suggestions for Further Reading

Jones, Beth Felker. *Practicing Christian Doctrine: An Introduction to Thinking and Living Theologically.* Grand Rapids: Baker Academic, 2014.

LaCugna, Catherine Mowry. *God for Us: The Trinity and Christian Life.* New York: HarperCollins Publishers, 1991.

Noble, Thomas A. *Holy Trinity: Holy People: The Theology of Christian Perfecting.* Eugene, OR: Cascade Books, 2013.

Placher, William C. *The Triune God: An Essay in Postliberal Theology.* Louisville: Westminster John Knox Press, 2007.

five
WHO IS JESUS CHRIST?

—∞∞∞—

Benjamin R. Cremer

Every Christmas, churches around the globe celebrate the birth of Jesus Christ. As the church calendar progresses, we mourn his death, triumph in his resurrection, and remain in awe after his ascension. As we look into the sky into which our Lord ascended, anticipating his return, and after we celebrate the coming of the Holy Spirit that Christ promised on Pentecost and the truth of the Trinity, we turn around and realize that Advent and Christmas are, again, just around the corner.

Year after year, we repeat the story of the life, death, resurrection, and ascension of Jesus. If this story were a TV show, we would be asking when season two was scheduled to begin. The season finale really left us in suspense, but after more than two thousand years, we would really like to know what happens next. Where is Jesus? Is he present with us? Or are we left waiting?

As much as we anticipate the second coming, there is a reason we continue to repeat the narrative of this one we call Immanuel, God with us. We are faithful to remember this story because of who Jesus is and how his first coming changed the world forever. It is more than just a story we tell; it is a story in which Christ invites us to participate, an unfolding plot in which we are to be characters.

In finding who we are in Christ, we can often take for granted the complexities of Jesus Christ's identity. We know we are saved from sin and its corruption through Jesus, but if we understand the magnitude of who Jesus is, we are better equipped to comprehend who we are as participants in the life and death through which God saves us. The fullness of who we are as Christians is revealed by traversing, through our Wesleyan lens, the profound identity of the one who has redeemed us.

Jesus Christ: Two in One

The Christian church confesses Jesus to be fully God and fully human, which is a complicated confession right off the bat. How is Christ at once both fully God and fully human? Did Christ's divinity overwhelm his humanity? Did Christ experience the depths of human suffering with both natures united? How we answer questions such as these reveals what we believe about the nature of Jesus Christ, and this is important work because what we believe about him shapes how faithfully we can live like him. We look like the Christ we worship and love.

Our culture highly favors individualism. So when we talk about the *person* of Christ, we often see him through the lens of autonomy—wholly separate unto himself. John Wesley helps us see how damaging that perspective is. Wesley understood the person of Christ as fundamentally relational. Siding with some of the church's earliest councils, Wesley saw that Jesus could only be fully known through his relationship to God the Father and his relationship to humanity.[1] As the Son of God, Christ is eternally one with the Father in heaven. Being sent to earth by the Father and born of the Virgin Mary, Christ is also the Son of Humanity. Jesus Christ's full identity is then understood in relation to both God and humanity in perfect equality. John Wesley held these two natures—God and human—together as the one person of Jesus, the Christ.

Understanding Christ as an individual separated unto himself is problematic. On the one side, we could fall into placing too much emphasis on Christ's divinity. Events such as his temptation in the wilderness, and especially his suffering in Jerusalem, could be seen as a cakewalk if Jesus only has a divine nature. One negative among many in holding this view is that we can begin to have a low view of the human body. If Christ was more God than human, then what happened to his earthly body is of little consequence. This perspective can have the tragic result of downplaying Christ's real suffering as well as our own. It is crucial to remember that Christ was not born, did not live, nor did he suffer, die, resurrect, or ascend into heaven *without* his body.

On the other side, if we overemphasize Christ's humanity, his ministry becomes the effort of his will alone, his miracles become a sort of magic, and his cross becomes only the loss of a noble, finite human being with no eternal impact. This perspective can cause us to see Christ's relationship with the Father as passive, at best, or manipulative, at worst. As a result, our relationship with God can be summed up by our own efforts; it can escalate to the extreme of attempting to manipulate God's power to our own benefit. To avoid pitfalls such as these, the person of Christ must not be confused with modern notions of the

---

1. For an excellent summary of how the Cappadocian Fathers and other ancient ecumenical councils shaped John Wesley's theology, see Kenneth J. Collins, *The Theology of John Wesley: Holy Love and the Shape of Grace* (Nashville: Abingdon Press, 2007).

isolated individual. The person of Christ *must* be understood as one who draws his very identity out of his relationship with God and humanity.

God for Us; Human on Behalf of Us

In his sermon titled "Spiritual Worship," Wesley points to the full character of Christ's divine nature by affirming that the Scripture writers gave Jesus all the titles of the Most High God. "They call him over and over by the incommunicable name, Jehovah, never given to any creature. They ascribe to him all the attributes and all the works of God. So that we need not scruple to pronounce him God of God, Light of light, very God of very God: in glory equal with the Father in majesty co-eternal."[2] We can agree with Wesley and with the Scripture writers that the same God who created the heavens and the earth is the one who took on flesh and dwelt among us.

It is this full expression of God in Christ that makes God's entry into our world all the more miraculous. The very spirit of the living God, through which everything was created, became flesh and dwelt among us as the Son of God (John 1:1–14). He took on flesh by being born of the Virgin Mary and became the Son of Humanity. Son of God, Son of Humanity. It is this coequal relation of divinity and humanity in the person of Christ that makes him more than capable of forgiving sin and restoring the connection between God and humanity (Mark 2:9–10). The one through whom the earth was created is the only one through whom the earth can be redeemed to its created purpose. What a miraculous event! The Most High God became a human like us out of love.

It is for this very reason that we the church return from looking up at the ascension year after year to remember anew the cycle of the birth, life, death, and resurrection as we await his return. We do so because we are a people who have been transformed by God's redemptive act on the cross. It is also by this faithful cycle of remembering the events of Christ's time on this earth that we acknowledge Christ's bodily presence. We have been commissioned by Christ to make him known in all the earth. The church is the evidence of Christ's first coming and continued ministry through and among his people. To be as faithful in our remembrance of Christ as he commanded us to be, we must not only be sure that he is not forgotten, but we must also be shaped and formed to live the life he lived—to be the body of Christ on earth here and now.

As Wesley reminds us, this necessary dynamic of holding together the divine and human natures in the one person of Christ keeps the character of God always before us. The God of the universe, the Creator of all things, is not a God

---

2. John Wesley, Sermon 77, "Spiritual Worship," in *Sermons III*, ed. Albert C. Outler, vol. 3 of *The Bicentennial Edition of the Works of John Wesley* (Nashville: Abingdon Press, 1976–), 90–91. Hereinafter abbreviated *Works* B.

who stays in the heavens, always out of reach. No, our God is a God of faithful love. Because of that faithful love, our God came down to us and, as Eugene Peterson puts it, "moved into the neighborhood"—our neighborhood (John 1:14, The Message). To know Christ is to know that our God will allow no boundary, divine or human, to hinder coming to us. For that reason we wait, we work in our various ministries, and we celebrate our Christian calendar year after year to remember who our king is and patiently anticipate his coming again. God's people will not be left on the cliffhanger of Christ's ascension forever. We serve a God who has come and dwelt among us. That God has promised to return and move back into our neighborhood again and dwell with us forever and ever. In the meantime, God is present here and now through the Holy Spirit.

Discussion Questions

1. How do you find yourself a participating character in the living story of the yearly cycle from Christmas to Christ's ascension into heaven?

2. How have you found it difficult to hold Jesus Christ's identity as fully God and fully human?

3. How have you seen the particular way you understand the person of Jesus Christ impact your Christian life?

4. In our endeavor to imitate Christ, in what ways do we as the church maintain Christ's mission? What ways can we as the church improve to be more like Christ?

Suggestions for Further Reading

Collins, Kenneth J. *The Theology of John Wesley: Holy Love and the Shape of Grace.* Nashville: Abingdon Press, 2007.

Pelikan, Jaroslav. *The Christian Tradition: A History of the Development of Doctrine: The Emergence of the Catholic Tradition (100-600).* Chicago: University of Chicago, 1977.

six

WHAT DOES THE HOLY SPIRIT DO?

Rhonda Crutcher

Once when I was a teenager, I was asked to fill in for the teacher of the senior adult Sunday school class at my little church in small-town Kansas. Every congregation has a class like this, consisting mostly of elderly ladies who have been in the church all their lives. I was eager to please, so I agreed. But, while preparing the lesson I began to doubt. What could I, an inexperienced sixteen-year-old, possibly teach these living saints? They should be the ones teaching me!

So it's not surprising that, in the classroom that Sunday, the tables were turned and the teacher became the student. As we talked about the work of God in the life of a believer, I found myself asking them questions, including the one that was paramount in my mind: *How does the Holy Spirit prevent you from sinning? Does the Spirit take over your will in such a way that you have no choice in what you think or do? If not, how does it work?*

I struggled with this question because I knew I was saved—and I was pretty sure I was sanctified—but I still sometimes had thoughts and desires that I knew were contrary to the Holy Spirit. *But once the Holy Spirit came into your life, you would never again want to act contrary to God's will, right? So I must not be sanctified, after all. Maybe I didn't pray hard enough during my last trip to the altar.*

This same conundrum has plagued many of us who have been raised in Wesleyan-holiness denominations, where the teaching of entire sanctification is emphasized. This confusion is often caused by poor understanding of the nature and work of the Holy Spirit, which is unfortunate since John Wesley's theology of the Spirit was robust and, properly understood, provides an answer to this common, perplexing question.

There are two main points about the nature and work of the Holy Spirit in Wesley's writings that are crucial in answering this and other common questions.

1. The Holy Spirit is a person, not a thing.

Just as it is important to speak of Christ as God, and in loving relationship with the rest of the Trinity, so too is it crucial to affirm, first and foremost, that the Holy Spirit is as equally divine and equally active in the love of the Trinity as the first two Persons. At times in the history of the church, the Spirit has been diminished or depersonalized or seen as subject to, or under, the Son. This misinterpretation is particularly problematic in Wesleyan theology, which leans in the direction of the part of the early Eastern church that was careful to emphasize the coequal and dynamic relationship within the Trinity. (See figures 1 and 2 in chapter 4.) Although it may be more difficult to use our imaginations to see the Holy Spirit as Person than it is the incarnate Christ, it is no less important. Admittedly, it is much easier to focus on the work of the Spirit than on the Spirit's nature because, as Jesus reminds us, we only see the wind through its effects.

The Bible often refers to the Holy Spirit as a gift that was given by Jesus to the disciples and later followers (cf. John 20:22; Acts 5:32; 8:18; Rom. 5:5; Gal. 3:5; 1 John 3:24). But this language should obviously be seen as a metaphor and does not mean that the Holy Spirit is a material *thing* that can be passed down from God to humans like a gift at a birthday party. Instead, we must balance this idea of gift with the many scriptures in which the Holy Spirit is portrayed clearly as a Person rather than a thing. In the New Testament the Holy Spirit *sends* (Mark 1:12); *leads* and *guides* (Luke 2:27; John 16:13; Rom. 8:14; Gal. 5:18); *speaks* (Mark 13:11; Acts 8:29; Gal. 4:6; 1 Tim. 4:1; Heb. 3:7); *teaches* (Luke 12:12; John 14:26; 1 Cor. 2:13); *testifies* (John 15:26; Acts 20:23; Rom. 8:16; Heb. 10:15; 1 John 5:6–8); *intercedes* (Rom. 8:26–27); and *acts* in other personal ways (Matt. 1:18, 20; Acts 15:28; 16:7). These are the distinct actions of a person, someone who has agency, not an object.

Wesley, who was nothing if not a student of the Scriptures, built on this biblical portrayal when he spoke about the Holy Spirit as a person who lives in relationship with the other persons of the Trinity, and with those who believe in Christ. Indeed, just as Christ was God *with us* in the incarnation, the Holy Spirit is now with us and in us as we wait for Christ's return. Christ did not leave us as orphans but sent the Holy Spirit to be actively present between the Advents. Mildred Bangs Wynkoop summarizes the Holy Spirit's personhood in her important work *A Theology of Love*: "The Holy Spirit is a Person and comes as a Person and He relates himself to persons. When one is saved the Holy Spirit comes to him. This is a **personal relationship**, not a mathematical addition which can be divided by fractions."[1]

1. Mildred Bangs Wynkoop, *A Theology of Love: The Dynamic of Wesleyanism* (Kansas City: Beacon Hill Press of Kansas City, 1972), 199. Emphasis added.

This is an important distinction because it allows us to understand the Spirit as a *living, dynamic* presence who leads Christians on the path of holiness rather than as an irresistible force who possesses us or whom we possess.[2] Christians maintain free will and still have the choice to ignore the Spirit's leading. At the same time, however, the Spirit is influencing and shaping the will of the Christian so that her or his will eventually becomes God's will as the person cooperates. In that sense, then, the Christian can eventually *want* to follow the direction and guidance of the Spirit but still has the ability to reject it.

However, like with all relationships, it is crucial that the Christian's relationship with the person of the Holy Spirit be nurtured. This is where devotions, prayer, sacraments, and other acts of spiritual discipline, or means of grace, come into play (see chapter 15). Wesley preaches,

> But if we do not then love him who first loved us; if we will not hearken to his voice; if we turn our eye away from him, and will not attend to the light which he pours upon us; his Spirit will not always strive: He will gradually withdraw, and leave us to the darkness of our own hearts. He will not continue to breathe into our soul, unless our soul breathes toward him again; unless our love, and prayer, and thanksgiving return to him, a sacrifice wherewith he is well pleased.[3]

So the performance of devotional actions in our Christian lives is not for show or to try to prove to God (or other people) how devout we are, or even to make God happy. Their purpose is to nourish and develop our relationship with the person of the Holy Spirit, who in turn transforms us into the very likeness of Christ.

2. The Holy Spirit is at the center of the work of our redemption, from beginning to end.

Another common way people can misunderstand the work of the Holy Spirit is to view it as something entirely absent in God's initial act of salvation—something that occurs as an add-on well after the person receives Christ as Savior. In incorrect theology in the past, the Holy Spirit was seen as active only in the work of entire sanctification (see chapter 13). This mistaken way of understanding second-blessing holiness (as it was called) unfortunately relegated the Holy Spirit to the role of a background player, lingering behind the scenes in the first act of salvation, waiting to appear on cue in the second act when the Christian desires to be entirely sanctified.

---

2. Wesley, Sermon 1, "Salvation by Faith," in *Sermons I*, vol. 1 of *Works* B, 75.

3. Wesley, Sermon 19, "The Great Privilege of Those That Are Born of God," in *Sermons III*, vol. 3 of *Works* B, 3.

However, the implication that the Holy Spirit has nothing to do with the initial drawing of the person to Christ, or in the actual act of salvation itself, or in daily life thereafter, is completely contrary to Wesley's teachings. Wesley emphasized the Holy Spirit's role through the entire process of the Christian's life, from the beginning of God's wooing in prevenient grace, through salvation or justification, and through progressive sanctification to life's end, and, of course, in what is called entire sanctification. It is simply wrong theology to believe that the Holy Spirit's only role is to deliver entirely sanctifying grace. "Hast thou received the Holy Ghost? If thou hast not, that art not yet a Christian."[4]

Indeed, for Wesley, the person and work of the Holy Spirit are first central to his idea of prevenient grace. He says,

> We are convinced, that we are not sufficient of ourselves to help ourselves; that, without the Spirit of God, we can do nothing but add sin to sin; that it is he alone who worketh in us by his almighty power, either to will or do that which is good; it being as impossible for us even to think a good thought, without the supernatural assistance of his Spirit, as to create ourselves, or to renew our whole souls in righteousness and true holiness.[5]

The person of the Holy Spirit makes humans capable of recognizing their need for God and repentance in the first place. Therefore, the Spirit's presence is the conduit through which salvation even becomes a possibility.

Therefore, Christians who have repented and have been reconciled to God *have already experienced the work of the Holy Spirit in their lives*, even from before they knew they needed salvation; and the Holy Spirit will continue to be present for their entire spiritual journey. The Spirit is not confined to the later stage of Christian perfection that begins at a moment of entire sanctification or infilling of the Spirit but is deeply present and active in the moment of salvation itself. Wesley refers to Christians as being "born again of the Spirit unto a new life which is hid with Christ in God."[6]

The Spirit's role, in Wesley's thought, also confirms this new-birth experience for us in what is called the Spirit's *assurance*. Wesley wrote extensively about the importance of the Spirit's witness or testimony to Christians to assure them of the saving (and, later, sanctifying) work of God in their lives, "the revelation of Christ in our hearts; a divine evidence or conviction of his love, his free, unmerited love to me a sinner; a sure confidence in his pardoning mercy, wrought in us by the Holy Ghost."[7] So the Holy Spirit is literally involved in every step and action of the work of salvation and the work of sanctification, from the initial call of the person

---

4. Wesley, Sermon 3, "Awake, Thou That Sleepest," in *Sermons I*, vol. 1 of *Works* B, 149.
5. Wesley, Sermon 17, "The Circumcision of the Heart," in ibid., 403-4.
6. Wesley, Sermon 1, "Salvation by Faith," in *Sermons II*, vol. 2 of *Works* B, 124.
7. Wesley, Sermon 17, "The Circumcision of the Heart," in *Sermons I*, vol. 1 of *Works* B, 405.

to the assurance of the effects of justification, in the progressive sanctification in daily Christian life, and before and after what is known as entire sanctification.

This, then, provides an answer to my teenage query about how the Spirit is at work in our lives. The Holy Spirit is an ever present and powerful agent in the ongoing work of reshaping us into the image of God. The Spirit does this not by taking over our wills so that we are automatically, unthinkingly manipulated into doing what God wants us to do. Rather, when the Spirit is regularly and properly unleashed, so to speak, through our cooperation with grace, God works in us to transform us—so much so that our choices are formed progressively to correspond to God's very purposes for us. This work of empowerment and transformation through the Spirit is what confirms to us the reality of God's presence operating in our lives—the same power that works through us to transform a needy world.

Discussion Questions

1. How have you typically thought about the work of the Holy Spirit in your life? Do you see it as a distinct action, separate from the initial work of salvation?

2. What actions do you take in your Christian life to nurture the Spirit? How do you see acts of spiritual discipline fostering this relationship? What actions are most meaningful to you?

3. In what ways do you see the Spirit working as a person in you rather than as a force?

4. How would you answer my question from that Sunday school class long ago, if someone asked it of you today?

Suggestions for Further Reading

Leclerc, Diane. "Mission Possible." In *Essential Church: A Wesleyan Ecclesiology*, edited by Diane Leclerc and Mark A. Maddix. Kansas City: Beacon Hill Press of Kansas City, 2014.

Shelton, Larry and Alex Deasley, eds. *The Spirit and the New Age.* Anderson, IN: Warner Press, 1986.

Stokes, Mark B. *The Holy Spirit in the Wesleyan Heritage.* Nashville: Abingdon Press, 1993.

PART 3
Creation, Humanity, and Sin

seven

HOW DID IT ALL BEGIN?

———— ∞∞∞ ————

Eric M. Vail

"Nothing comes from nothing / nothing ever could." Maria and Captain von Trapp sing these lyrics to each other in Rodgers and Hammerstein's *The Sound of Music*. The logic found in these lines goes back to the ancient world. From zero comes zero. No cookies come out of an empty cookie jar. Maria and Captain von Trapp are so certain that "nothing comes from nothing" that they conclude, "so somewhere in my youth or childhood / I must have done something good." The unlikelihood that they would ever experience love from another person like this must have an explanation from something that already existed.

While ancient Greek philosophers explicitly said, "Nothing comes from nothing," authors from the ancient Semitic world of the Hebrew people did not exactly talk in that way. They would not necessarily have disagreed if asked, yet they were less abstract. In talking about where things come from, Semitic authors did not talk about *something* and/or *nothing*. They just talked about the opposite circumstances of what we have now. We have light; the world must have once been dark with no lights in the heavens. We have land that sticks out above the waters; the land must have once been under the waters. We know of land putting forth plants; the land must have once been unproductive. The land, air, and seas are currently full of inhabitants; they must have once been empty. These circumstances before God's creative work are not *nothing* in the precise way the Greeks understood the term.

We are so accustomed to saying that God created "out of nothing" (*ex nihilo*) that the Semitic way of talking about creation (used by Old Testament authors) is jarring to us. They assume there was stuff there to work with; it is simply not arranged as we would expect. It is functionless. The earth is a dry, barren place at the start of Genesis 2:4 because so many things have not yet happened to make the world like we know it. Genesis 1 also contradicts the idea of nothing; after the introductory thesis statement—"In the beginning God created the heavens and the earth" (1:1)—we are told in verse 2 what the earth was like before God does anything—"now the earth was . . ." It is "uncultivated wilderness" (*tohu*) and "empty" (*bohu*). At the surface are the deep waters and darkness (not unlike Psalm 104:6).

Christians did not start to shift from this Semitic way of talking about creation out of primordial conditions until the middle of the second century. At that time, Christians began to adopt a new way of talking about creation that pushed back against the Hellenistic notion of world formation from unoriginated material;[1] but this shift away from creation as formation then differed from the culture of Israel represented in the Bible. Over several centuries, more Christians stopped talking about God *forming* (i.e., creating or making) our world out of some primal milieu of stuff and began to discuss it in terms of our now standard claim that God created everything *out of nothing*.[2]

There are several reasons for the transition to the doctrine of creation out of nothing. One reason is our monotheistic belief that nothing else can have divine status. God alone is everlasting, with no beginning or ending; everything else is dependent on God for existence (not just form and function). If material stuff has no beginning, it too would be everlasting, in the same way that God is everlasting. It is possible to imagine that God everlastingly gives existence to the material stuff out of which all things are formed.[3] (That is a better option than having matter eternally existing on its own, leaving us with a dualism between two eternal, uncreated entities.) Nevertheless, there is a theme in the Scriptures regarding a beginning point; for example, "The LORD brought me [Wisdom] forth as the first of his works, before his deeds of old; I was formed long ages ago, at the very beginning, when the world came to be" (Prov. 8:22–23). This passage refers to a period "before his deeds of old . . . long ages ago, at the very beginning." This language suggests there is a starting point—a beginning—to God's generative deeds. Creator is not one of God's eternal attributes. At some point God started bringing forth and sustaining all there now is—"the heavens and the earth." Only God is everlasting.

---

1. Among Gnostic thinkers in the second century there was a growing discussion about world formation within the categories of Hellenistic thought. This pressed more orthodox-minded Christians to wrestle in new ways with the doctrine of creation in light of these encroaching movements.

2. A key resource that explains the transition in the Christian doctrine of creation over Christianity's first few centuries is Gerhard May, *Creatio Ex Nihilo: The Doctrine of "Creation Out of Nothing" in Early Christian Thought*, trans. A. S. Worrall (Edinburgh: T&T Clark, 1994).

3. See Thomas Jay Oord, "God Always Creates out of Creation in Love," in *Theologies of Creation: Creatio Ex Nihilo and Its New Rivals*, ed. Thomas Jay Oord (New York; London: Routledge, 2015), 109–22.

A second reason for the doctrine of creation out of nothing is related to the first. The Bible affirms the goodness of God's material creation (Gen. 1:31) and creation as God's temple/dwelling place. God established and will ultimately redeem all things (Rev. 21:5). If God is the originator of material creation, then God's goodness undergirds everything that comes into existence. By the nature of its existence (coming to be in/out of the love of God), the world can be a natural home for God as God's glory shines throughout. If material stuff does not owe its existence to God, then God's goodness would have to be a foreign additive to a more natural or primal way that matter exists.

Some Greek philosophy was happy to accept that being part of the material world was a *bad* thing and that humans needed to escape our physical embodiment in order to be eternally spiritual. The Scriptures do not allow Christians to think that way (although some have tried!). God created humans to be physical beings, and being immersed in a physical world is good. In Judeo-Christian thinking, sin is not a *natural* part of life in God's creation but, rather, a continued perversion against God's own creative, sustaining activity (see chapter 8). Sin is not deeper down or further back into our existence than the goodness of God, in whom "we live and move and have our being" (Acts 17:28); sin is the intruder, not goodness. Any deviance to the way we interact with God and neighbor in love will be rectified, and God will evermore make God's dwelling among us (Rev. 21:2–7). Thus, in order to eliminate any dualistic idea that there is an eternal struggle between God and anything material (like the Gnostics believed), Christians came to strongly affirm that our good, holy God is the Creator of a good, material world. It is only our blasphemous rejection, in the interim, of God's ever active gift of love that is the problem.

Other facets of God's nature and activity were at issue in moving to the doctrine of creation out of nothing, in early church history and beyond. First was the issue of God's power or ability. Was God limited to use only what is already available to God? Was God constrained within the parameters of possibility already set by the quantity and quality of what existed? Is this universe nothing more than the best God could form out of the stuff that was floating around? This would reduce God to something like a child in a complex sandbox. Ultimately, was God able to make a creation as God saw fit, or was God inhibited by available resources? The capacities of a God who can bring the world into existence out of nothing far exceed the capacities of a God limited by fixed resources.

Furthermore, to say that there was primordial stuff coeternal with God puts the limit of God's will and freedom at issue. For example, are the properties of the various elements and forces in physics something God thought up and desired, or are they just the way things were because that is what stuff is like eternally? If stuff is eternal, and if God has to work within the givenness and fixedness of matter's attributes that exist eternally alongside God, God would be the beneficiary (or casualty) of some blind fate that precedes and supersedes God's own will and activity. God would be stuck in a cosmos with qualities not of God's choosing. In such a circumstance, it would be difficult to parse out what in the universe we should thank God for doing, and what we should thank matter for because it just happens to be the way it is. Perhaps, instead, we would be left to thank *fate* because we and God are ultimately bound to do our best under its confines.

Here is the beauty of moving from creation out of something to the doctrine of creation out of nothing. God's power (or capacity to act) supersedes the confines of reality. Rather than God existing and working eternally from within a reality that is given *to* God, a reality in which matter is a part, God *precedes* and *supersedes* all realities of created existence. As the Nicene Creed proclaims, God is indeed almighty as Creator of all there is—both things visible and invisible. The sum total of all things does not (and cannot) stack up beyond the reaches of God or exhaust the generative capacities of God. Even if all things go awry or run out, God cannot be overwhelmed. Furthermore, the features of our universe are the handiwork of God: To God alone be all honor, glory, and praise. It is within this creation and through this creation that God's love can be expressed radiantly. God wisely and willfully created all things such that God's will could indeed be done on earth as it is in heaven.[4]

The best part of creation out of nothing is that everything is a gift. The universe does not have to exist. God elected that there would be something and not nothing. God lavishly chose that there would be a good something with wondrous things to see, hear, smell, taste, and touch. (God also graciously gave us a world where we would be alerted to trouble by unpleasant appearances, noises, odors, flavors, or sensations.) God chose to create something that God could gift to us for us to enjoy—the reception and expression of the very love that God eternally shares among the persons of the Trinity (see chapter 4). The answer to the question, *Why is there something instead of nothing?* is: *Because God is love.* Out of love, God gives. And the answer to the question, *Why are various properties this way instead of another way?* is: *Because God is love.* The loving God gives good gifts.

In the beginning, before the beginning, as the possibility of a beginning, God is—period. There is impossibility for anything else to erupt ungenerated, except through God. Creation does not emerge based on enough passage of time or on the innate properties of elements and physical forces. Creation and God's creatures will not continue to exist eternally based on innate properties of any feature of creation. God alone is the one factor standing between nothing and

---

4. Wherever pure love is not expressed in the nurture of others, it is not God's action. Rather, this is creation's blasphemous response to God's initiating activity—thus, a sin against God, self, and neighbor.

something, between impossibility and possibility, between death and life—"the Spirit of God was hovering over the waters" (Gen. 1:2). God alone is the giver of life. And God is the sustainer of life. There is no other hope than God alone.

Recently, there have been criticisms of the doctrine of creation out of nothing. One criticism is that this doctrine is not biblical; it is a later development within Christianity. While detailed scholarship can show that to be true, creation out of nothing is nevertheless consistent with the underlying point that Hebrew writers are making: Apart from God, any creation, any life, would be impossible. The point the biblical authors are making is more about God, and far less about our belief that there is primordial, ungenerated stuff. We do not have to keep that ancient, Near Eastern view of the world any more than we have to keep the biblical idea that the sun revolves around the earth.

A second recent critique of creation out of nothing actually contradicts the core of Wesleyan thinking, which is that love is God's central attribute, *not* sovereignty. This second critique depicts God's action as being absolute and unquestionable. In other words, the critique says that God speaks all things into being exactly as God wills them—which leaves us to accept the form of our existence as the sovereign will of God, whether that is good or agonizing or even evil. Again, according to the critique, everything comes into being as it does because God spoke it into being that way. In this scenario, all problems would lie at God's feet—even sin. Thus, this critique of creation out of nothing is dependent on the idea that in creation, God determines all that follows. This idea of creation by dictate does not leave much room for the strong Wesleyan understanding of free will that includes creaturely responsibility for the ills in the world. If the reason for this second critique is that the concept of creation out of nothing necessitates a view of God that is unrelational and predetermining, Wesleyanism itself can critique this critique!

Wesleyans believe that God is love. Because of the emphasis on love over sovereignty, we do not say God saves by sovereign dictate but, rather, by enabling our cooperation. Why would we have two versions of how God acts? Why say that in creation God can be as dictatorial as God wants but, in other areas, proclaim that God is love? There is a way to keep consistency of God's character *and* affirm creation out of nothing. While it is true that there are Wesleyan scholars who go too far and reject creation *ex nihilo*, Wesleyan theology is, for the most part, able to maintain free will and the loving character of God without reducing God's creative strength.

If we look again at Genesis 1, God invites more often than God barks during creation: "Let the water" (vv. 9, 20); "Let the land" (vv. 11, 24). Even the commands of God—"Let there be"—are preceded by the hovering presence of the Spirit of God (v. 2). The Spirit's prevenient presence at creation makes it possible for that which is not to step forward into true being and existence, in response to God's creative call. As creation comes into existence, it is doing so *in response* to God's loving call.[5] In a very similar way, the Spirit's prevenient grace makes it possible for us to leave our lives of sin and death as we are called to come into true being and existence—indeed, new life in God. In this new life, we are called to act like God (even creatively) as we love God and neighbor freely. In a sense, when we love, we reestablish the created order that God designed when it was unaffected by sin and fallenness.

We Wesleyans should learn to talk about creation out of nothing not as some ancient event that holds little relevance for our lives but according to our emphasis on divine love that invites our present cooperation in the restoration of all things.

Discussion Questions

1. What attributes of God are affirmed by claiming that creation happens out of nothing? How might this understanding of God shape the way we live before God and engage God in worship or prayer?

2. What attributes of creation and creatures are affirmed by claiming creation out of nothing? How do these attributes of creation shape our imagination about sin and the possibility of holy living in the world?

3. The author suggests that God is consistent in interacting with creation through enabling response to God's initiating call. How do we explain how God can be a good Creator, even though there is sin in the world? In what way does God's method of creating make our very existence in the world a heavy responsibility?

Suggestions for Further Reading

Brown, William P. *The Seven Pillars of Creation: The Bible, Science, and the Ecology of Wonder.* Oxford; New York: Oxford University Press, 2010.

Kaiser, Christopher B. *Creational Theology and the History of Physical Science: The Creationist Tradition from Basil to Bohr.* Studies in the History of Christian Thought. Vol. 78. Leiden; New York: Brill, 1997.

May, Gerhard. *Creatio Ex Nihilo: The Doctrine of "Creation out of Nothing" in Early Christian Thought.* New York: T&T Clark, 2004.

Oord, Thomas Jay, ed. *Theologies of Creation: Creatio Ex Nihilo and Its New Rivals.* New York: Routledge, 2015.

Walton, John. *The Lost World of Genesis One: Ancient Cosmology and the Origins Debate.* Downers Grove, IL: IVP Academic, 2009.

---

5. See my book *Creation and Chaos Talk: Charting a Way Forward* (Eugene, OR: Pickwick Publications, 2012) or "Creation out of Nothing Remodeled" in *Theologies of Creation*, 55-67.

eight
WHAT DOES IT MEAN TO BE HUMAN?

―∞―

Ryan L. Hansen

"What are human beings that you are mindful of them?" (Ps. 8:4, NRSV). So begins the psalmist in a meditation that is not first, or ultimately, about the human person but is, rather, about God. This fragment about humanity is set within the whole sweep of theological vision—placed in the context of God's majesty and glory, God's superabundant gift, God's sheer creative energy in the world—from newborn babies to distant stars and everything in between. It is as if the singer wishes to sing about the human person but must begin and end by speaking of the glory and splendor of God. This impulse instructs us; those whose understanding of humanity is being shaped by Scripture recognize that to speak of the created human person is not to speak of that person as self-possessed and in isolation, thrown out into the world as self-sufficient and whole. Rather, to speak of human persons is to speak of ones who have been related to by a God who is their Creator, Redeemer, and Restorer. Basically, the human person is a relation, in relationships, with God and with neighbors and with other living creatures. Thus, rather than saying that human persons have potential (as if their true being comes from something inside of them), it is perhaps preferable to say that human beings have a capacity for relationships (*capacity* in the sense of room or space in which to welcome others).[1]

But this understanding creates a puzzle. Humans are designed to have a relationship with God, but it seems, at the same time, that this same capacity for relationship is also the condition for human frailty and sinfulness. Scriptural witness suggests that the human person is created to be turned toward God in relationship, but it also shows frailty and a sinful tendency to turn away from

---

1. Craig Keen, "Homo Precarius: Prayer in the Image and Likeness of God," *Wesleyan Theological Journal* 33 no. 1 (1998): 142–46.

God. The human person is always bodily and earthy (created from dirt, after all) but is designed to be so as related to the life-giving God. Christians confess that what it means to be human in this way cannot be understood apart from the one who was most truly the human One—the crucified and resurrected Jesus Christ.

Human Existence in the Old Testament

The biblical creation account describes humans as ones created in the image of God (Gen. 1:26–27). This concept is often understood to mean that the human being possesses some innate quality that is (at the least) analogous to one of God's qualities: creativity, reason, the divine spark, and so on. This approach sees the human individual, standing whole and self-possessed, *having* something that makes the person like God in some way; ergo, one could draw a straight line from a human quality to a divine quality.

However, when Genesis speaks of humans created in the image of God, it sets this insight within the larger vision of creation. God creates by a word that desires and enables response: "Let there be." God does not zap everything into place unilaterally but makes everything with the capacity to respond (1:20, 24). The earth is not created by producing something out of its own potential to put things forth but as a response to the creative word and call of God. The image of God is like this as well—not a possession of the human's but a response to the divine word and call.[2] The image of God *is* the relationships in which the original humans find themselves; we are also now in the image of God because God still calls us to relationships. The question is whether the image is distorted because our relationships are not as they were created to be.

In the creation accounts in Genesis, this relational basis of human existence is further emphasized. There, God forms the humans out of the dust of the earth and breathes life into their nostrils. The Hebrew terms used here are unique and enlightening. First, the word for breath is *něshamah*, which means breath. This is the life-giving empowerment from God that brings life to the human person. This life is the movement of God to lifeless dirt. It is this movement that creates the person and that unsettles the dust and turns the creature back toward God.[3] To be human is to be turned and moved toward the God who turns and moves toward us. But the scriptural story also reminds us that this vision of the divine-human

---

2. Claus Westermann, *Genesis 1-11: A Commentary*, trans. J. J. Scullion, S.J. (Minneapolis: Augsburg, 1984), 148–58. Westermann writes, "The creation of humanity has as its goal a happening between God and human beings . . . it is not a question of a quality in human beings . . . God has created all people 'to correspond to him,' that is, so that something can happen between creator and creature" (158).

3. Hans Walter Wolff, *Anthropology of the Old Testament* (Mifflintown, PA: Sigler Press, 1996), 32–39.

relationship is fractured and frustrated. Because the human person is essentially needy—hungry for God—if the person is turned away from God to other things or turned in on the self, that person becomes frail and infirm, disempowered, and ultimately sinful.

The sinful condition is characterized by an existence oriented not toward God's empowerment but toward self and things (or persons) of the world.[4] Apart from God's breath, "all flesh would perish together, and all mortals return to dust" (Job 34:15, NRSV; cf. Ps. 104:27–30). It seems that the condition of being needy for God is what makes the human vulnerable to frailty and turning away. To be created for genuine relationship means that relationship can also be refused. Sin, therefore, is not a loss of the image of God in the person (since it was never a true possession to begin with) but a disconnect in the relationship between God and the human (or between humans, or between humans and other creatures).

Humanity in the New Testament: The Relation Restored

These terms and ideas become the fundamental framework for some of the New Testament writers' thinking about what it means to be human. For Paul, humanity exists in a state of existence he calls "flesh" (*sarx* in the Greek). Paul here is not talking about flesh as skin or as physical existence versus disembodied, spiritual existence. Flesh is a condition of being turned away from God, imprisoned by the powers of sin and death. The human oriented toward flesh is deathly, but God in Christ has acted to give God's Spirit (*pneuma*) or God's *breath* of new creation life, not just to rescue the person from the condition of being "in the flesh" but to create that person anew (2 Cor. 5:17). This is all accomplished through Christ, whom Paul envisions as the perfect human, the example and empowerer of a new way of being human, and the last (or final) Adam (Rom. 5:12–21; 1 Cor. 15:20–28, 45–49; 2 Cor. 5:14–21). Jesus, *the* quintessential human, is the one who opens up a new way to *be* human, healing the relation between God and humanity. Not only does Jesus display the living hunger for God that humanity was created to show (Phil. 2:7), but he is also the one who breathes the divine life into humans. As Paul writes, "'The first man, Adam, became a living being'[5]; the last Adam became a life-giving spirit [*pneuma*]" (1 Cor. 15:45, NRSV).

It is as this bridge figure between God and humanity that Christ is the exemplary human. Christ is the relational connection between God and humans and is the fully human one whom people are to reflect. Colossians calls Christ

---

4. Ibid., 26–31.

5. Paul here is quoting from Gen. 2:7 in the Septuagint, which translates *nephesh* ("living being") as *psyche* in Greek.

the "image of the invisible God" specifically because he is both Creator (God's movement toward creation) and Reconciler (creation's responsive movement toward God): "For in him all things in heaven and on earth were created . . . and in him, all things hold together . . . and through him God was pleased to reconcile to himself all things" (Col. 1:15–17, 20, NRSV). Christ can be said to be the image of God precisely because he has this relation between God and humanity in himself.

Elsewhere, the writer of Hebrews draws on Psalm 8 to present Christ as the one who, despite the rest of humanity's failure to live into God's vision of relationship, has made the voyage of the truly human and stands crowned in God's presence with glory and honor (Heb. 2:5–9). Christ is the perfect human one who makes a journey to God to clear the path for the rest of humanity to enter into God's salvation, a newly created and restored human existence—living in the reality of the defeat of sin and death and in deep relationship and friendship with God (Heb. 2:10, 12:2). For the New Testament writers, then, it is impossible to think of humanity without thinking of the person and work of Christ.

Wesley's Understanding of Humanity

John Wesley's theological anthropology (doctrine of humanity from a theological perspective) was deeply formed by these biblical frameworks. The Christian—and particularly the Wesleyan—conviction is that the fullest reality of human existence is deeply relational. Being a human means to open up to the God who pours out God's very self in love for humanity (and all creation). And a person open to God is also open to her or his neighbor. A relationship with God and neighbor is not an optional add-on to what the human person is; rather, it is part of the essence of being human. Similarly, the image of God does not reside in the human person; it is what happens as God and the human person face each other in love.

For Wesley, the human person is designed to be God's counterpart. This belief is confirmed in the fact that humans are created in the image of God.[6] However, the emptiness that makes the human person needy for God is also the very thing that can make the human run off course, pursuing other loves (idols). Even so, the fact of humanity's fallen condition only amplifies the depths of

---

6. Though in his sermon "The Image of God" Wesley seems to regard the image as a set of characteristics residing within the person—namely understanding, love, and liberty—they are generally spelled out in fundamentally relational terms. Understanding corresponds to God's way of understanding creation, love was the human's "vital heat . . . continually streaming forth, directly to him from whom it came" (*John Wesley's Sermons*, 15-16). Only liberty remains a kind of self-possession for Wesley.

God's pursuit of God's creation.[7] God's love to fallen humanity only confirms that humanity is designed for relationship with God and others. The God and human relationship is demonstrated, for Wesley, nowhere more clearly than in the person and work of Christ. Christ is the supreme expression of God's love. Christ's work restores humanity in the image of God. The person perfected in the love of Christ is seen by Wesley as having a perfect openness to and being outgoing toward God (and neighbor). In an insightful passage Wesley prays,

> For what is the most perfect creature in heaven or earth in Thy presence, but a void capable of being filled with Thee and by Thee; as the air which is void and dark, is capable of being filled with the light of the sun, who withdraws it every day to restore it the next, there being nothing in the air that either appropriates the light or resists it?[8]

Elsewhere, Wesley shares his vision of the life of the human restored by Christ:

> [It] implies the continual inspiration of God's Holy Spirit: God's breathing into the soul, and the soul's breathing back what it first receives from God; a continual action of God upon the soul, and re-action of the soul upon God; an unceasing presence of God, the loving, pardoning God, manifested to the heart, and perceived by faith; and an unceasing return of love, praise, and prayer, offering up all the thoughts of our hearts, all the words of our tongues, all the works of our hands, all our body, soul, and spirit, to be an holy sacrifice, acceptable unto God in Christ Jesus.[9]

And so, to speak of the human person is not first, or ultimately, to speak *about* the human person but about God. To speak of humans is to speak of the God who created them, who pursues them to the depths of sin and death, who restores them in Christ, and who empowers their love to overflow back to God and to neighbor. The human person can never be spoken of apart from God because, in Christ, God has so bound God's self up with humanity that they can never be separated (Rom. 8:31–39).

One might think that a chapter on humanity should follow a chapter on sin, in light of the above discussion of Christ's healing of the divine-human relationship—indeed, the healing of sin. But it is important to recognize that the human being is *not* essentially sinful. That is, humans in the condition of sin, as ones turned away from God, are distorted away from their original, relational design. It is only *after* this is made clear, and *after* we are reminded of the hope we have in Christ, that a chapter on sin is appropriate.

---

7. Wesley, "God's Love to Fallen Man," in *John Wesley's Sermons*, 477–84.

8. Wesley, *Plain Account of Christian Perfection*, 113.

9. Wesley, "The Great Privilege of those that are Born of God," in *John Wesley's Sermons*, 191.

Discussion Questions

1. In light of this chapter, why is it important to say that humanity is created and sustained by God?

2. What is the image of God, according to this author's interpretation?

3. In what sense are we like Christ in our humanity?

4. Review the Wesley quotes in this chapter. How do they help us understand what it means to be human?

Suggestions for Further Reading

Keen, Craig. "Homo Precarius: Prayer in the Image and Likeness of God." *Wesleyan Theological Journal* 33, no. 1 (1998): 128–50.

Moll, Rob. *What Your Body Knows About God: How We Are Designed to Connect, Serve, and Thrive.* Downers Grove, IL: InterVarsity Press, 2014.

Wesley, John. "God's Love to Fallen Man." In *John Wesley's Sermons: An Anthology,* edited by Albert C. Outler and Richard P. Heitzenrater. Nashville: Abingdon Press, 1991.

———. "The Great Privilege of those that are Born of God." In *John Wesley's Sermons.*

nine
HOW DO WE DEFINE SIN?

———⟨∞∞⟩———

Diane Leclerc

If theology is primarily about God and God's relationship with humanity, then any full-orbed discussion of theology must pay attention to the significant break of relationship between God and humans—namely, sin. Likewise, if the theology of holiness is the main emphasis of the Wesleyan-holiness theological tradition and the goal of Christian life and practice, sin must also be thoroughly considered as the greatest threat to holiness. While much of theology formed early in the church, sin took much longer to define historically; it does not show up in the ecumenical councils or creeds, except in the phrase "I believe in the forgiveness of sin"—perhaps because it would seem that sin should be self-evident and obvious to us.

But even today there are various interpretations of what sin is. There are differences among theological traditions when answering questions such as the following: *What is at the heart of sin? Are there different categories of sin? What is original sin, or inherited depravity? Is sin inevitable? How does the work of Christ and the Holy Spirit affect sin, and what can we hope for in this life?* We will try to answer these types of questions as an attempt to gain more clarity about sin, for if we lack clarity on this topic, we can also misunderstand the topics of salvation and sanctification and the related topics of the church and its mission in the world—all connected, of course, to the meaning and purpose of the Christian life as love, and all threatened by the destructive nature of sin.

The doctrine of sin, called *hamartiology*, divides sin into three main categories: personal sins, original sin, and systemic evil. The first two will be addressed in this chapter, systemic evil in the next.

Personal Sin

By personal sin, we mean the acts done by individuals. There are many ways to define personal sin. The original Greek word literally means to "miss the mark," as if aiming at a target and missing. Some have simply called sin disobedience against God. For others, it is "fall[ing] short of the glory of God" (Rom. 3:23); for still others, the willful transgression of a known law of God.

One of the key issues that separates different traditions is the question of whether sin must always be intentional or volitional. This determination is vital to decide when attempting to define sin. One tradition's perspective defines sin more broadly than what a person *chooses* to do. Sin does not have to be a willful act for John Calvin but includes the multiple ways we fall short of God's intentions, such as lack of wisdom, poor but innocent (by way of ignorance) choices, mistakes, and imperfections common to being human. Calvin's understanding of sin is wide. It is no wonder, then, that Calvin implies that sin is inevitable and will persist throughout the whole Christian life. He is working with a different definition of sin.

The question of what constitutes sin is one key place where Wesleyans and Calvinists disagree. Although Wesleyans sometimes define sin perhaps too narrowly, in general we do affirm that people are aware that they are sinning when they do. Sin is a willful act in the Wesleyan theological paradigm. When Wesley considers such realities as imperfections, or what he calls *infirmities*, he believes these to be amoral. In other words, there are behaviors that are neither moral nor immoral. It is possible for our actions to be amoral—meaning that some actions fall short of absolute human perfection, but God does not hold us morally responsible for such limitations. (These would include physical disabilities or mental illnesses, for example.) Rather, God holds us accountable only when we comply with sin, when we choose to participate in sin, when we give in to temptation and harm our relationship with God or others *willingly*.

This does not mean, however, that we are not still responsible when we harm one another unintentionally. When we hurt a spouse or friend unknowingly, and they point it out to us, our response should not be, "Well, I'm not responsible because I didn't mean it!" Our love and commitments to each other should surely lead us to genuine sorrow and apologies, despite the innocence of our will. In a similar way, even though God might not hold us eternally accountable for unintentional acts, the same sorrow and confession should be our loving response to God when we miss the mark inadvertently. Such love and responsiveness is at the heart of every relationship, especially when it is damaged.

So Wesley labeled imperfections, infirmities, and unintentional failures as "sin improperly so called." If Wesleyans exclude these from a definition of sin, it makes much more sense when we affirm that sin is *not* inevitable, necessary, or perpetual in the Christian life. We believe that forgiving and sanctifying grace is greater than the power of sin! "Sin properly so called" implies willfulness, yet the Holy Spirit can help us be victorious over such willfulness as we grow in our sanctification, character, and love, and as God purifies the intentions of our hearts.

But when we deliberately break the laws of God—those that are specified, written down, and those written upon our hearts—we sin. Such "properly so called" sins are further categorized as sins of *commission*. When we break the laws of God or the law of love by doing things we shouldn't, we commit sin.

There are also sins of *omission*. James makes it very clear that "if anyone, then, knows the good they ought to do and doesn't do it, it is sin for them" (James 4:17). James addresses several problematic issues of the day in his short epistle. For instance, the original readers show favoritism to the rich and neglect the poor. They know that the right and good thing to do would be to feed the hungry and lift up those who are oppressed. But they choose not to do it. They *omit* the good, and sin.

Such sins of omission show us another important reason we should live confessional lives before God. There is need all around us. It is impossible for us to spend every moment fulfilling the needs of the whole world. But we do need to be in tune with the Holy Spirit in order to be led to specific situations where God wants us to intervene. When we don't obey in those instances, according to James, we sin, and need to confess. It is obviously impossible to address every need in every moment. We *will* fall short. We will sin by omission. This fact should still bring us humbly before the throne of grace, even if we were never to commit a "thou shalt not."

Another aspect of the doctrine of sin is to ask an essential question about personal sin, whether commission or omission: *How do we know sin when we see it? Is there a way to identify sin as such? What is at its essence?* It is too easy to think of the Ten Commandments as arbitrary laws. In other words, we could believe that God randomly chose ten things to prohibit so that humans would know when we had displeased God and so we would always remember that God is God and we are not. If this is as deep as we go in our thinking, we might imagine that one of the ten could just as randomly be, "Thou shalt not wear purple socks." If we did decide to wear purple socks, then we would be sinners—simply because God commanded us not to. The sole way to determine what sin is would be to memorize all the prohibitions that God fashioned, as the Pharisees do when they obey the 613 laws listed in the Old Testament. But this is a limited and nearsighted way to look at sin.

In reality, when we examine the Ten Commandments, and all of the laws given by God, we will see that each commandment is *relational*, even the ones that no longer culturally apply (like the prohibition on eating pork). First of all, we affirm that God gave the commandments because God first loved us—God knew that breaking a command is ultimately detrimental *to us*. Sin destroys. Further, all of the commands, even the hundreds beyond the Ten Commandments, reference actions that go against love—whether love of God, of others, or even of ourselves (i.e., eating undercooked pork could make us very ill). Regarding the Ten Commandments, when we worship other gods or graven images, we cease to love God, and turn away with our hunger for God toward inadequate idols that can never satisfy us. When we steal, or murder, or bear false witness, we cease to love each other. This understanding is why Jesus can so strongly say that when we truly love God with all of our being and our neighbors as ourselves, *we fulfill the whole law*. This explains why he also says that our righteousness must exceed the righteousness of the Pharisees. The Pharisees obeyed the 613, but they missed the point of love.

Indeed, to really love as God desires, our love must go beyond a legalistic understanding of the law as determining right and wrong. Love is the measure of our Christian ethics (see chapter 14). So when we come across situations where "there is no law," we can still discern the wisest course of action if we pursue true *agape* love. In sum, we can say that sin is, at its essence, anti-love, and that love, at its essence, leaves no room for sin. This articulation is why Wesley used the phrase "love excludes sin." If the heart is filled with love, there will no longer be room for sin. The contrary image of a heart filled with sin brings us to original sin.

Original Sin

Before the year 386, the theology of sin focused almost exclusively on personal sin, emphasizing the freedom of the human will. After 386, one of Christianity's greatest converts, Augustine, developed ideas about *why* we sin in the first place. His reflections stem from Genesis and the story of the fall, the origin of sin entering into the pristine world God created; Augustine interprets the scene in the garden. He also reflects on his own life and his struggle with sin, and identifies with Paul's reflections in Romans 7, where he describes sin acting as a master over him before he met Christ.

Augustine's thoughts are also formed by encountering the writings of a British monk named Pelagius. For Pelagius, the only effect of the fall on the future of humanity is that it brought mortality to humans. The sin of Adam and Eve caused death to enter into the world so that every human being thereafter would die. Again, this is the *only* effect for Pelagius.

Augustine believed that there are more consequences from the fall than just death. He began to argue that all generations after Adam and Eve would inherit a sinful disposition. This inherited depravity affects every human being ever born (except Jesus). Therefore, when Augustine pondered the question of why we sin, he concluded that human beings sin because we are born with a sinful nature. Free will is, in a sense, lost. We are only *free* to sin, according to Augustine. These ideas came to be known as the doctrine of original sin. The doctrine was affirmed to be true, and Pelagius was labeled a heretic, at the Council of Orange in the year 529, although the council did not affirm everything that Augustine believed to be necessarily true (such as his strong view of predestination).

John Wesley also believed in original sin but did not agree with Augustine entirely. Besides rejecting predestination, Wesley added his doctrine of *prevenient grace* to the understanding of original sin. Prevenient grace has many functions in the world, including the belief that the Holy Spirit is at work in every person's life by drawing, or wooing, her or him into a relationship with God. Wesley also used prevenient grace to explain that, even though everybody is born with original sin, everyone is also given a grace that restores free will. This clarification is important because, without a gracefully restored free will, no one could be justly held accountable for her or his sins (and predestination must therefore be affirmed). If original sin compels me to sin against my will, then how is God just in holding me accountable for doing something I cannot help but do? Prevenient grace allows us to answer this question. While Wesley holds strongly to a doctrine of free grace from the moment we are born, he also affirms that we continue to be influenced toward sin by *reigning sin* (his preferred phrase for original sin), even in the Christian life.

The idea of reigning sin becomes very important in Wesley's discussion of holiness and sanctification (see chapter 13). In disagreement with his Moravian friends, Wesley finally concludes that people are not entirely sanctified at the moment they are converted to Christ. In other words, even though all *past* sins are forgiven by the atoning grace of God received at the new birth, the sinful disposition remains and can even *reign* in the Christian life. It requires the deeper work of God through sanctification to replace sin in a Christian's heart with love. Indeed, to be entirely sanctified is to allow love to *reign,* again, so that love might exclude sin.

Does this doctrine make it impossible for Christians to sin after they are entirely sanctified? Wesley was asked this question often. In Wesley's mature theology, he came to believe that sanctified Christians could certainly sin! To believe otherwise would be to place ourselves above Christ, for we must maintain that Christ was truly tempted and was truly *able* to sin (although he didn't). More to the point, Wesley concluded that an absolute, godlike perfection of sinlessness is not possible in this life. (Remember our discussion of the sins of omission.) But he did optimistically affirm that our dispositions and our character can be so radically changed by grace that we sin less and *want* to sin less, as we abide in Christ. Even more to the point, holiness should not be equated with sinlessness. We should not define holiness by using the idea of the *absence* of sin. I could be sinless and still not be holy! How? Holiness must have a positive content. Holiness must be defined as the *presence* of perfect love (Christlike and God-given *agape* love), not as the absence of sin. I may avoid sin altogether, but if I have not love, I am nothing.

If we go back to Augustine, we will find that he not only affirmed original sin but also defined it. The very essence of sin for Augustine is pride. Much of Western Christianity has adopted this definition. Wesley, however, is more nuanced. Wesley often defined the essence of sin as *idolatry*. My understanding of Wesley has led me to believe that defining the essence of original sin *only* as pride is inadequate.

Examine the diagram below.

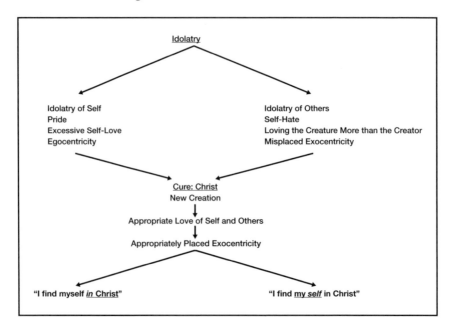

For Wesley, sin is idolatry. Idolatry can express itself in two ways. On the left side of the diagram, we see a well-known description. Sin has most often been portrayed as pride, egocentricity, or self-love. These are ways to describe an idolatry of self. Those who are egocentric destroy relationships through their own self-absorption. But some scholars of Wesley, and even of the early church, recognize another way to express sin seen in Christian history.[1] There is an expression of sin that is rather opposite to the words on the left.

On the right side of the diagram, we recognize that idolatry of others can also dominate. Loving the creature more than the Creator is a biblical idea

---

1. See Diane Leclerc, *Singleness of Heart: Gender, Sin, and Holiness in Historical Perspective* (Lanham, MD: Scarecrow Press, 2001), for historical figures whose work contributed to this view, including Jerome, Chrysostom, John Wesley, Phoebe Palmer, and Søren Kierkegaard.

(Rom. 1:25) that Wesley often employed. If egocentricity is a form of sin, then the opposite sin is misplaced exocentricity (outside oneself)—meaning, finding oneself only in the love of another human being (or in drugs, money, power, etc.). This type of sin causes a person to be completely dependent on others for her or his identity. This can lead to self-hate, even self-loathing. It also destroys relationships. Idolatry is not God's intent for people. Sometimes we get humility and self-hate mixed up. God wants us to be humble but only after God empowers us to *have a self* that we then can give up in love.

As the diagram shows, the cure for both idolatry of self and idolatry of others is Christ alone. In Christ we are created anew. We find our identity in Christ's love and sacrifice for us. Our exocentricity is *appropriately* placed in God. As God writes God's name on our hearts, and as we allow God to reign in our lives, only then are we able to love ourselves and love others appropriately. We find ourselves in Christ. For some, as those on the left, finding themselves *in* Christ is emphasized as they reorient their egocentric selves toward God. For those on the right, finding *themselves* in Christ is emphasized as they experience the very birth of a self that God has loved.

In sum, sin is anti-love. It damages and even devastates relationships. Personal sins, whether of commission or omission, keep us from being all that God has created us to be, as individuals and in relationship with God and others. God hates sin because it destroys us, whom God loves. We also affirm that beneath our personal sins is original sin as a damaging influence. It damages the image of God within us. Yet, through new birth and sanctification, we can live into the love of God that dwells within us, as God restores our original image. We do not have to live in bondage to sin through our entire earthly lives. Wesleyan optimism is founded on the incredible grace of God that changes and transforms us from the inside out.

Discussion Questions

1. What is the difference between personal sin and original sin?

2. Why do you think we seldom hear about the sin of omission? How can we know sin when we see it?

3. Wesleyan theology affirms that sin is intentional or willful. In what sense are we responsible for unintended acts that damage our relationships?

4. What does Wesley mean by "sins improperly so-called"? How does this understanding help us in our compassion for others?

5. Wesley affirms original sin as idolatry. Which side of the idolatry diagram do you lean toward? How is Christ the cure for all original sin?

Suggestions for Further Reading

Boone, Dan. *Seven Deadly Sins: The Uncomfortable Truth.* Kansas City: Beacon Hill Press of Kansas City, 2008.

Callen, Barry L. and Donald Thorsen, eds. *Heart and Life: Rediscovering Holy Living.* Lexington, KY: Aldersgate Press, 2012.

Mannoia, Ken and Donald Thorsen, eds. *The Holiness Manifesto.* Grand Rapids: Eerdmans, 2008.

Key Wesley Sermons:

"Spiritual Idolatry"

"Original Sin"

"On Sin in Believers"

"The Repentance of Believers"

ten

WHAT IS SYSTEMIC EVIL?

—∞∞∞—

Sarah Whittle

The term *systemic evil* refers to the idea that evil, including the expression in humans of anti-God activity, is not merely a problem with the human condition—and thus a matter of guarding personal, individual piety—but is a systemic and corporate problem. That is, evil does not exist merely in the human heart but is a cosmic and spiritual reality that exercises its power through our institutions and is entwined with our day-to-day lives to the extent that we no longer recognize it for what it is. The language of "spirits and powers" is not something that parts of the church are familiar or comfortable with; nonetheless, we need to take seriously the voice of Scripture, especially considering our Wesleyan understanding of corporate holiness.

Three manifestations of evil have been observed in Paul's letter to the Ephesians, according to which, in 2:1-2, believers are no longer "dead in the trespasses and sins [personal evil] in which you once walked, following the course of this world [systemic evil], following the prince of the power of the air [cosmological evil], the spirit that is now at work in the sons of disobedience."[1] From this text: First, the flesh is described as the human inclination to sinning at a *personal* level. Second, the ways of the world are also evil, representing the *systemic* level. Third, the devil represents the *cosmological* influence of evil, described in terms of the prince of the power of the air.[2] Scripture has a clear picture of evil and anti-God power perpetuated by nonhuman agents; they can be evil and can bring about evil.

---

1. Fletcher L. Tink, "Conflict," in *Dictionary of Scripture and Ethics*, ed. Joel B. Green (Grand Rapids: Baker Academic, 2012), 163–64.

2. Ibid.

We see in Paul, for example, a sense of sin as coconspirator with evil, and as cosmic power.[3] We are urged not to consider sin "strictly as a feature of human activity or human experience."[4] It is not only a transgression, a human disposition or flaw of human nature; rather, as Beverly Gaventa points out, Sin (in a sense personified) "came into the world" (Rom. 5:12, NRSV); sin "increased" (5:20); sin "exercised dominion" (5:21; cf. 6:12, 14, NRSV); sin "produced" (7:8, NRSV); sin "revived" (7:9, NRSV); sin "dwells" (7:17, 20, NRSV). "It is an uppercase Power that enslaves humankind and stands over against God. . . . Sin is among those anti-God powers whose final defeat the resurrection of Jesus Christ inaugurates and guarantees."[5]

Now back to the systemic level. "The world" relates to created institutions, often taken-for-granted ways of being, which may over time become self-serving, oppressive, and damaging—perpetuating systemic evil. "This world" or "this age" is a negative category in the New Testament, referring to a way of being—of persons and systems—that is conformed to the evil around it. Those involved are unable to do anything about it because they are unable to recognize it for what it is—evil. They follow the evil one, or the prince of the power of the air. But they have now been "made . . . alive together with Christ" (Eph. 2:5, NRSV). Similarly, Paul urges the church in Rome not to "be conformed to this *world*, but be transformed" (Rom. 12:2, NRSV, emphasis added). In this sense, salvation is not merely a matter of personal morality but a matter of having moved from obedience to the powers who operate in this world, deceiving the children of darkness, to new life in Christ, who has ultimate victory over these powers.

Walter Wink has described the dominating systems of "the world" or "this age"—to put it in biblical terms—as characterized by hierarchy, rank, and polarities: They involve power exercised over others, social organization as control of others, hierarchies of dominance and subordinance, winners and losers, insiders and outsiders, honored and shamed. Wink sees these powers driven by their quest for domination—and these come to pervade the social order, often without our awareness. Many of us, even Christians, are willing to conform to these powers and their anti-God purposes to the extent that it is difficult for us to imagine, let alone take steps to create an alternative. This willingness is dangerous and damaging.

Such systemic evil is evident in economic and political structures—and the church is not exempt. There are systems that privilege the already wealthy and perpetuate injustice, gender discrimination, racism, militarism, and a lust for power. Wink talks about "the myth of redemptive violence" as a particularly

---

3. Beverly Roberts Gaventa, *Our Mother Saint Paul* (Louisville; London: Westminster John Knox Press, 2007), 125.
4. Ibid., 126.
5. Ibid., 127.

pervasive power.[6] In this dominating system, violence becomes the solution to all human conflict. Children are socialized into violence, and humans respond to others in increasingly violent ways. Senseless violence becomes normalized, even as an option for Christians. Wink says of these systems:

> These constitute the "power of the air," the invisible but palpable power of opinions, beliefs, propaganda, convictions, prejudices, hatreds, racial and class biases, taboos, and loyalties that condition our perception of the world. It kills us precisely because we breathe it in before we even realize it is noxious. Like fish in water, we are not even aware that it exists, much less that it determines the way we think, speak, and act.[7]

But as Jesus defeats these powers at the cross, Paul identifies himself writing from prison as "seated . . . in the heavenly places in Christ" (Eph. 2:6, NRSV). This juxtaposition of suffering and victory marks Christian Scripture. Exaltation as victory over the powers of the world comes about by self-giving and suffering rather than armed victories; in the defeat of evil, battle imagery remains metaphorical. The energy of evil must be transformed. As Paul puts it, "Do not repay anyone evil for evil" (Rom. 12:17). Paul was aware that repaying evil with evil merely perpetuates evil—giving more power to the powers. Ultimately, Christ is over all the powers, and we participate as Christ brings them under his Lordship. Christ brings the kingdom and kingdom values. But we must participate in Christlike ways.[8]

Angels, demons, and cosmic struggles: Do these represent some primitive, superstitious belief, and what should we think about them now? Jesus teaches his disciples to pray "deliver us from the evil one" (Matt. 6:13), the one whom Jesus himself has, of course, already resisted. In the exalted Christology of Ephesians, Christ is superior to all the heavenly powers (Eph. 1:21; cf. Col. 1:16). There is an "angelic" leader of these hostile powers—"the ruler of the power of the air" (Eph. 2:2, NRSV), the devil (Eph. 6:11), and humans who do individual or sociopolitical evil are inspired by such "angelic" power.[9] By way of response, Ephesians urges believers to "stand against the schemes of the devil. For we do not wrestle against flesh and blood, but against the rulers, against the authorities, against the cosmic powers over this present darkness, against the spiritual forces of evil

---

6. Walter Wink, *Engaging the Powers: Discernment and Resistance in a World of Domination* (Minneapolis: Fortress, 1992), 13–31. Wink describes the myth of redemptive violence as the "foundational myth" of the domination system.

7. Walter Wink, *Naming the Powers: The Language of Power in the New Testament* (Minneapolis: Fortress, 1984), 84.

8. Rom. 8:38; 1 Cor. 15:24; Eph. 1:20–22, 3:10, 6:11–12; Col. 1:16, 2:8–10, 15; Phil. 2:10; 1 Peter 3:22.

9. Pheme Perkins, *Ephesians*, in *Abingdon New Testament Commentaries* (Nashville: Abingdon Press, 1997), 51.

in the heavenly places." Believers are exhorted to "take up the full armor of God, that you may be able to withstand in the evil day" (Eph. 6:11–13, ESV). So there is a strong argument to make for taking this language and these ideas seriously, uncomfortable as it may be.

Paul reflects on the corporate solidarity of humans after asserting that "all have sinned" (Rom. 3:23). He traces the entry of sin into the world to Adam; all have sinned because all are in Adam. Thinking of sin merely as personal deficiency in terms of relationship with God, ensuring our personal redemption, guarding our own salvation is not enough. A mark of Wesleyans is that conceptions of holiness are social and corporate. We stress the importance of community for becoming Christlike; holiness is worked out in and among those to whom we are called to belong. The idea of systemic evil matters for this sense of corporate holiness, for just as we are corporately responsible for supporting each other's growth in holiness, so too we must be corporately responsible for guarding against that which would hinder human flourishing and the life of God—within and outside our communities. So we must always consider the impact of our actions on our neighbors in the broadest sense.

The idea that believers are somehow protected from evil's deceptive power is false. On one hand, the eschatology of the New Testament describes our relationship with sin and the powers as being dead to sin and exalted with Christ above all principalities and powers. On the other hand, it repeatedly warns that evil and sin and the other anti-God powers are deceptive and pervasive and that we must be aware of them and choose to live justly and rightly, in holiness and purity. Being in Christ is not a magical formula but a powerful assertion of a change of allegiance on the basis of the victory over sin and death in which believers will ultimately fully participate. But it requires our awareness.

As one author points out, our missteps may be due to a failure of knowledge rather than a failure of love. But the doctrine of systemic evil places this failure of knowledge in a new and sinister light: Our failure of knowledge concerning the systemic evils in which we are implicated is by no means simple ignorance; rather, it is "false consciousness," a deeply rooted failure to recognize evils, whose recognition would cost us something.[10] For example, we *might* be unconscious about the racism around us. But, more often than not, we turn our eyes away because to really recognize it would mean that we ourselves must resist and fight it.

The antidote to this peril of thought is to take a different view of the world, a view rooted in Scripture, in some of the hard sayings about giving and generosity, about wage justice, about welcoming the stranger or immigrant, about nonviolence and justice for the oppressed, and to consider who benefits and who

---

10. William Hasker, "Holiness and Systemic Evil: A Response to Al Truesdale," *Wesleyan Theological Journal* 19, no. 2 (1984): 62.

suffers from our everyday interactions. Scripture presents us with a countercultural view of the world. It is clearly something we are required to practice here and now, in the present evil age.

As one writer puts it, "How we talk about sin influences what we will *do* about it."[11] Thus it is important to recognize that evil can be seen in relation to power, exercised by heavenly or earthly rulers and authorities and pervasive in political, economic, and social structures. Consequently, we will need discernment to see evil for what it is, and we will need to ask hard questions about whether the way in which we read Scripture and live our lives means that we are really resisting evil or implicitly colluding with the systems by which evil is perpetuated. Systemic evil affects all of us, implicating us in sin and wrongdoing. It requires our perception and commitment to action.

To try to think through the intricacies regarding systemic evil as it relates to personal responsibility takes us immediately into the mire. We will participate in evil systems no matter how conscious and aware we are. We can resist greed, for example, but when we buy anything, we may be oppressing others economically in the world. It is here that we must ask God for wisdom and discernment. Do we boycott particularly irresponsible companies, for example? It is impossible for us on our own to fight all oppression in the world. But as members of Christ's church, it is important to cultivate sensitivity to issues such as these and to seek ways to corporately oppose the powers of this world. Overall, we are to see through Christ's eyes and work against any and all dehumanization, as the enemy of God's design and purposes in the here and now and for all eternity.

Discussion Questions

1. How does the idea of systemic evil challenge the definition of sin as a willful transgression of a known law of God?

2. In what sense are we responsible for the evil systems in which we participate? What are some ways we can resist evils like discrimination, economic oppression, and dehumanization?

3. In what sense has Christ already overcome the world? How is the church supposed to act in response to institutions of evil, such as political and economic systems?

4. Define and discuss "false consciousness."

---

11. Gary A. Anderson, *Sin: A History* (Newhaven and London: Yale University Press, 2009), 13.

Suggestions for Further Reading

Anderson, Gary A. *Sin: A History.* New Haven, CT; London: Yale University Press, 2009.

Hasker, William. "Holiness and Systemic Evil: A Response to Al Truesdale." *Wesleyan Theological Journal* 19, no. 2 (1984).

Tink, Fletcher L. "Conflict." In *Dictionary of Scripture and Ethics,* edited by Joel B. Green, 163–64. Grand Rapids: Baker Academic, 2012.

Wink, Walter. *Engaging the Powers: Discernment and Resistance in a World of Domination.* Minneapolis: Fortress Press, 1992.

———. *Naming the Powers: The Language of Power in the New Testament.* Minneapolis: Fortress Press, 1984.

eleven
IF GOD IS GOD, WHY DO WE SUFFER?

———— ⨯ ————

Joe Gorman

My twenty-year-old daughter, Annie, has a progressive and chronic bone disease called progressive pseudo-rheumatoid condra dysplasia. The disease mimics rheumatoid arthritis and has complications such as scoliosis, deteriorating joints, osteoporosis, stunted growth, and chronic and sometimes overwhelming pain. Annie has had seven major surgeries and many other so-called minor procedures in the past fifteen years. Some of these have helped relieve her pain; others have inflicted more suffering. Today she is able to walk short distances, thanks to double hip and knee replacements and hundreds of hours of physical therapy. Even though these surgical procedures have "given me my life back,"[1] as Annie says, she daily experiences chronic pain and other limitations.

I hesitate to mention Annie's story because I do not want to objectify, exploit, or trivialize her pain. Her life is not merely an object lesson from which others can learn how to suffer well. Yet I cannot separate my journey with her suffering from my relationship with God or my theological reflections on why there is suffering in God's good world—especially for children. Because Annie and too many others I love suffer in various ways, I will never be a detached, third-person bystander when it comes to suffering. Suffering is not a puzzle to be solved for me. It has a face. It has a name. Perhaps it does for you as well.

Theodicy

Theology, as the study of God, helps us to engage seriously the most vexing and personal questions of life, including, *Where is God when I and those I love suf-*

---

1. Annie and Joe Gorman, "Cupcakes and Compassion," *Nazarene Compassionate Ministries Magazine* (Spring 2013): 19–21, accessed March 31, 2016, http://content.yudu.com/Library /A22wfk/NCMMagazine-Spring201/resources/3.htm.

fer? How do we reconcile the existence of the all-loving, all-powerful God of Christian Scripture with accidents, illnesses, genetic disorders, and random violence that occur in God's good world? The attempt to answer such questions is called *theodicy* by philosophers and theologians.

Theodicy comes from the Greek words *theos* (meaning God) and *dik* (meaning justice). Thus, it literally means to justify God. Theodicy seeks to explain how the existence of a good and powerful God can be justified in a world in which so many suffer for no apparent reason. Many theologians, like Stanley Hauerwas, for example, question whether theodicy is a legitimate endeavor for Christian theology: "It is speculatively interesting to ask how the existence of a good and all-powerful God can be reconciled with the existence of evil in the world. . . . But when I confront the actual suffering and threatened death of my child—such speculative considerations grounding belief or unbelief seem hollow."[2]

Free Will

Much that we call evil may be explained through the misuse of human free will. Wars, accidents, poverty, ignorance, errors of human judgment, and, of course, sin account for much of human suffering—but not all of it. A couple years ago, in my state of Idaho, a mother was accidentally killed by her two-year-old son while they were shopping after Christmas.[3] The mother had a concealed-weapons permit, and when she turned her back for just a moment, the toddler reached into his mother's purse, found the gun, and tragically shot and killed his mother. Free will is a wonderful gift, but this is an example of a gift gone tragically wrong.

We may speculate as to why God did not prevent this horrible accident, but a pastoral-theological approach asks: Where is God in such a situation? A pastoral-theological perspective assures us that God is comforting the toddler, helping first responders bring order out of chaos, and beginning a lifelong process of healing a traumatized family and community. One thing is clear, however: God did not cause this mother's death. Free will may help explain logically how such a heartbreaking accident may occur, but if we think that free will alone can make the absurd intelligible, we are asking it to do more than it can do.[4]

2. Stanley Hauerwas, *Naming the Silences: God, Medicine, and the Problem of Suffering* (Grand Rapids: Eerdmans, 1990), 1.

3. See Terrance McCoy, "The Inside Story of How an Idaho Toddler Shot His Mom at Wal-Mart," *Washington Post*, December 31, 2014, accessed March 31, 2016, http://www.washingtonpost.com /news/morning-mix/wp/2014/12/31/the-inside-story-of-how-an-idaho-toddler-shot-his-mom-at-wal-mart/.

4. Hauerwas, *Naming the Silences*, 73.

Natural Evil

We may also wonder about the origin of what are often called natural evils, such as viruses, tsunamis, earthquakes, tornadoes, hurricanes, and volcanoes. Such natural evils are not necessarily evil, however, for there is a sense in which earthquakes and the like are thought to be part of an incredibly complex planetary system that makes possible the conditions necessary for the flourishing of life on earth.[5] We perceive them as evil when they encounter, and often devastate, human life. Natural evils may also be seen as the groans of creation itself that reverberate between initial creation and creation's final consummation in a new heaven and new earth (Rom. 8:22; Rev. 21:1). Still others suggest that the persistence of natural evils is the result of a creation "wounded . . . in its uttermost depths . . . by a primordial catastrophe."[6]

As helpful as these explanations of so-called natural evils may be for some, I do not find them personally or pastorally comforting when I think of Annie's bone disease or friends or of family members who have terminal illnesses or of children with genetic disorders. What we need in the face of suffering is compassionate response rather than theoretical explanation. As Nicholas Wolterstorff observes in the aftermath of his son's tragic death, "Instead of explaining our suffering, God shares it."[7] However we seek to understand natural evils, there is no definitive or completely satisfying answer for why these evils persist. Rather than trying to provide an explanation for such evils, we will do well to remember that the purpose of Scripture is not to tell us why these things happen but to affirm God's constant work to redeem evil and suffering (Rom. 8:28). As the ministry of Jesus reminds us, God calls us to join in the alleviation of human suffering rather than to speculate about its causes (Luke 13:1–5).

Divine Power and Presence

A common response to tragic events is sometimes expressed in the bumper-sticker platitude "Everything happens for a reason." While the sentiment behind this statement seeks to make sense of God's presence and power in the midst of suffering, the slogan itself actually expresses a toxic theology. Is there really any morally acceptable reason why children suffer? What moral logic can possibly be extracted from the death of a child? If everything happens for a reason—that is, is part of a meticulous, predetermined divine plan—then this makes God responsible for everything that happens—including sin, evil,

---

5. Thank you to my good friend Steve Smith, a geologist with the United States Geological Survey, who first suggested this idea to me many years ago.

6. David Bentley Hart, *The Doors of the Sea: Where Was God in the Tsunami?* (Grand Rapids: Eerdmans, 2005), 22, 62.

7. Nicholas Wolterstorff, *Lament for a Son* (Grand Rapids: Eerdmans, 1987), 81.

and suffering. In this "blueprint"[8] view of God, God becomes a torturer and murderer of children. When someone understands God this way, he or she may understand pain and suffering as a message—or even punishment—from God. This, however, is not the God we see in Christ (John 9:1–3) or the God affirmed in the Wesleyan theological tradition.

Wesleyan theology rejects the idea that God predetermines everything, like a divine puppet master, where humans are merely dolls on a string. Wesleyan theology understands God's power differently. Rather than hoarding power, we believe God shares power with us so that we may partner with God in God's redemptive purposes.[9] God's power, according to Wesleyans, is most perfectly manifested not in a meticulous, predetermined, divine blueprint but in Christ's vulnerable, suffering love on the cross. What we believe theologically about God's power has tremendous implications for how we understand and respond to suffering. While we may submit to a God of absolute power and control, it is difficult to trust, let alone truly love, a God who treats us as puppets rather than beloved children.

Prevenient Grace

A Wesleyan theology of suffering also stresses that God's redemptive love is everywhere. Because God's goodness indwells all creation, there is literally nowhere that God is not. This divine characteristic is commonly called *omnipresence*. Wesleyans often refer to it as prevenient grace. So where is God when unimaginable suffering and evil strike? Trinitarian theology affirms that it is the very presence of the Trinity—Father, Son, and Holy Spirit—with the abused, the trafficked, the sick, and the attacked to save, sustain, heal, and renew all things in Christ. Such divine, loving presence "means that the Spirit was in Auschwitz's fiery pits of burning children, in the eye-melting heat of the Hiroshima blast—and most particularly, hanging on the cross of Jesus."[10] A robust Trinitarian theology helps us to see God in places our tear-stained eyes alone cannot see (Ex. 6:9; Luke 24:13–35; John 20:11–16).

Soul-Making

Another way Christians seek to make sense of evil and suffering is to speak of the good that can come from suffering (Rom. 5:3–5). This practice is called soul-making theodicy. While growth in faith, hope, and love may develop as

---

8. Gregory A. Boyd, *Is God to Blame? Beyond Pat Answers to the Problem of Suffering* (Downers Grove, IL: InterVarsity Press, 2003), 41ff.

9. Michael Lodahl, *The Story of God: A Narrative Theology*, 2nd ed. (Kansas City: Beacon Hill Press of Kansas City, 2008), 62.

10. Ibid.

a result of faithful suffering, this result does not explain why suffering occurs. Speaking in the wake of the mountain-climbing accident that led to the death of his son, Wolterstorff writes:

> Suffering may do us good—may be a blessing, something to be thankful for. This I have learned. . . . How can we thank God for suffering's yield while asking for its removal? In the valley of suffering, despair and bitterness are brewed. But there also character is made. The valley of suffering is the vale of soul-making. How do I receive my suffering as blessing while repulsing the obscene thought that God jiggled the mountain to make *me* better?[11]

Wolterstorff's insights caution us to think carefully about what our theology of soul-making says about our understanding of God. To say that God allows rape, for example, in order to strengthen the soul of the victim makes God a devil. And who could possibly believe in a God who allows a child to be born with a terminal genetic disorder only so that the child and that child's parents can be an inspiration to others?[12] Even though unimagined good may come from suffering—and we must honestly acknowledge that sometimes it does not—this never makes extreme suffering *worth it*. Cannot growth come through far less painful and tragic means? There simply is no moral algorithm that can ever fully explain the loss of a loved one, let alone the suffering and death of millions.

A Churchly Theodicy

Theodicy may seem like a reasonable enough pursuit when viewed from the outside looking in; but when it's your suffering or that of a loved one, especially a child, endlessly seeking after theoretical explanations often leads to bitterness rather than comfort. For pastoral-theological reasons I find theoretical theodicies to be of limited value in a Christian theology of suffering. There simply is no logical formula that solves the problem of evil. Various theodicies have helped me grasp the philosophical considerations involved in understanding the tensions that arise when affirming the existence of a loving and powerful God in the face of evil, but they alone do not fully satisfy, theologically or personally. Rather than grounding my faith in the logic of theodicy, I place my hope instead in the God who suffered on the cross and raised Christ from the dead.

At present we are saved in hope (Rom. 8:24). We yearn and lament[13] for definitive answers to the problem of evil yet see only so far: "For now we see in

---

11. Wolterstorff, *Lament for a Son*, 97.

12. In her poignant TED Talk "I'm Not Your Inspiration, Thank You Very Much," Stella Young calls this "inspiration porn," accessed March 31, 2016, http://www.ted.com/talks/stella _young_i_m_not_your_inspiration_thank_you_very_much?language=en.

13. For an important resource on lament as a means of grace especially in times of suffering, see Walter Brueggemann, *The Message of the Psalms* (Philadelphia: Fortress Press, 1985).

a mirror, dimly, but then we will see face to face. Now I know only in part; then I will know fully, even as I have been fully known" (1 Cor. 13:12, NRSV). But even through what is often a "cloud of unknowing,"[14] or mystery, we affirm that "faith, hope, and love" do indeed "remain" (1 Cor. 13:13a). It is the presence of the suffering/resurrecting One in the church who sustains the Christian virtues of faith, hope, and love even in the midst of inexplicable suffering. As Stanley Hauerwas affirms: "Historically speaking, Christians have not had a 'solution' to the problem of evil. Rather, they have had a community of care that has made it possible for them to absorb the destructive terror of evil that constantly threatens to destroy all human relations."[15] Hauerwas's churchly response to suffering reflects my family's and my journey with Annie's bone disease. The church, as a means of grace,[16] makes the unbearable bearable.

Our local church, rather than trying to explain the why of Annie's suffering, prayed for us, visited us at home and in the hospital, and brought meals to us. Their incarnational presence fostered hope when we were tempted to despair. They mourned and rejoiced with us (Rom. 12:15). We sat together in darkness on Good Friday. We rejoiced together at the empty tomb of Easter morning. We sang together songs of hope. We prayed together. We cried and lamented together. We celebrated weekly Communion together. We engaged in redemptive ministry to the suffering together.

Churchly means of grace nurture faith, hope, and love as well as assure us of God's presence even when we or loved ones suffer for seemingly no good reason. For this reason a biblical response to evil and suffering always looks and acts like the body of Christ.[17] In a church that lives under the shadow of the cross and leans into the sunrise of the resurrection is found the kind of community in which the suffering are made welcome, pain is embraced, and where companioning and incarnational presence, rather than easy answers and false comforts, are offered. Until the fullness of the kingdom comes, we labor in hope together for the day when God will raise up all who have suffered and "wipe every tear from their eyes. Death will be no more; mourning and crying and pain will be no more, for the first things have passed away" (Rev. 21:4, NRSV).

---

14. See the spiritual classic by the same title written by an anonymous fourteenth-century English monk: *The Cloud of Unknowing* (San Francisco: HarperCollins, 2004).

15. Hauerwas, *Naming the Silences*, 53.

16. For John Wesley's explanation of the means of grace, see his sermon "The Means of Grace," in *Sermons I,* vol. 1 of *Works* B, 376-97. Broadly understood, means of grace are those practices, habits, relationships, and experiences that mediate God's grace and lead to love of God and neighbor.

17. Whenever I think of what the church is called to be, I think of the Golden, Colorado, Church of the Nazarene, where I was the senior pastor for almost twenty-one years. Even though I was the pastor, they shepherded my family and me during some of the most difficult times of our lives.

Discussion Questions

1. When have you experienced the church as a means of grace when you or a loved one has suffered? What means of grace have sustained you or a loved one when you have experienced devastating loss? How can you and your church be a means of grace to those who suffer in your local community and world?

2. Our theology informs our response to those who suffer. As we represent Christ to the suffering, what are we to say or not say? How do we know which actions are helpful or hurtful in such a situation? Begin to develop on your own or in a small group a pastoral-theological response to those who suffer.

3. Interact with Wolterstorff's advice to those who minister to the suffering: "If you can't think of anything at all to say, just say, 'I can't think of anything to say. But I want you to know that we are with you in your grief.' Or even, just embrace. Not even the best of words can take away the pain."[18]

4. What difference does it make for understanding and responding to the problem of evil and suffering if we read Scripture through a Wesleyan, Calvinist, or other theological lens?

Suggestions for Further Reading

Hauerwas, Stanley. *Naming the Silences: God, Medicine, and the Problem of Suffering.* Grand Rapids: Eerdmans, 1990.

Stump, Eleonore. *Wandering in Darkness: Narrative and the Problem of Suffering.* Oxford: Oxford University Press, 2010.

Truesdale, Al. *If God Is God Then Why? Letters from New York City.* Kansas City: Beacon Hill Press of Kansas City, 2002.

Wolterstorff, Nicholas. *Lament for a Son.* Grand Rapids: Eerdmans, 1987.

---

18. Wolterstorff, *Lament for a Son*, 34.

PART 4

Saved and Sanctified

twelve

WHAT DOES IT MEAN TO BE SAVED?

※

Jacob Lett

The central theme of Scripture, the heart of the gospel, and the emphasis of Wesleyan theology is that humanity finds its salvation in Jesus Christ. The doctrine of salvation addresses how the person of Christ (Christology) and the work of Christ (atonement) reshape and transform not only humanity but also the entire cosmos. All religions and cultures teach some form of salvation or human transformation. Yet, according to Wesley, it is precisely the belief of salvation in Jesus Christ that differentiates Christianity from other religions.[1] It is also the doctrine of salvation that is at the very heart of Wesleyan essentials.

There is no final definition of salvation. Christians and Christian thinkers have always understood there to be a mysterious nature to salvation that cannot be explained fully. Scripture itself does not provide a single definition that accounts for all dimensions of salvation but makes use of a host of metaphors. Yet there is a particular focus in Scripture and in the better parts of church history about the very center of salvation's possibility. Stated concisely, Jesus Christ is more than a person who came to proclaim the character of God's salvation. Rather, Jesus Christ *is* salvation. He *is* the Savior. Through his life, death, resurrection, and ascension, salvation has come to the created order. In Scripture, Paul uses the phrase "in Christ" seventy-three times. Most of these references refer to a multitude of images on the nature of Christ and his work of salvation.[2] Therefore, if one claim can be made about the doctrine of salvation, it is that it occurs "in Christ."

From this foundation, how do Christ's death and resurrection transform humanity? What has changed and is changing due to the work of Christ? Unfor-

---

1. John Wesley, *The Letters of the Rev. John Wesley*, ed. John Telford, 8 vols. (London: Epworth, 1931), 3:332–70.

2. Constantine Campbell, *Paul and Union with Christ* (Grand Rapids: Zondervan, 2012), 67, 328.

tunately, some evangelicalism in America has reduced salvation to the "sinner's prayer," prayed when believers accept Christ into their hearts. Yet, as Wesley notes in his sermon "The Scripture Way of Salvation," salvation is much wider and refers to "the entire work of God, from the first dawning of grace in the soul till it is consummated in glory."[3] In other words, for Wesley, salvation includes the entire Christian life, not just the initial moment of belief. The transformation of humanity in the person of Jesus Christ can be categorized into the three stages of reconciliation, new birth, and participation. These three categories are traditional ways of understanding how the atonement (referring to what Christ did on the cross) affects humanity. The full work of salvation involves all three,[4] though Wesleyan theology especially places its emphasis on the final category of *participation* "in Christ."

Reconciliation

Scripture clearly speaks of an abyss between God and humanity (Eph. 2:12). There could be no other result to a world of corporate and personal sin than separation and alienation from God. Reconciliation, then, is the re-creation of broken fellowship. It is the transformation and elimination of the abyss. How does this transformation occur? Second Corinthians 5:19 (NRSV) states, "In Christ God was reconciling the world to himself."

How can one person reconcile all humanity, though? If Jesus was *merely* human, he could not accomplish this on humanity's behalf. It is only as God that Christ could undertake to represent all humanity before the Father (see chapter 5). Only a divine being could be the "last Adam" who creates the possibility of a new race (1 Cor. 15:45). At the same time, it is only by becoming fully human that God could do for humanity what humanity could not do for itself (Rom. 8:3; 2 Cor. 5:21). Therefore, in Christ, one finds a double representation. Only the *God*-man could represent all humanity before God, and only the God-*man* could transform humanity.

By consuming the very alienation between God and humanity and dying on the cross, Jesus delivers humanity from the consequences of sin. Humanity is no longer alienated but has "peace with God" (Rom. 5:1). Fellowship has been restored. The "wrath" against sin has been averted (1 Thess. 1:10). It is important to note that in a Wesleyan theology God's wrath is not toward the individual *per se*, but toward the sin that so negatively affects the individual whom God loves. In this sense, one can speak of the corporate and cosmic nature of wrath and sin, in the

---

3. John Wesley, Sermon 43, "The Scripture Way of Salvation," in *Sermons II*, vol. 2 of *Works B*, 156.

4. These three are also not all-inclusive to what happens in salvation through the atonement. Other important events include justification, adoption, redemption, and initial sanctification.

same way one understands the corporate and cosmic nature of salvation (Col. 1:20). Christ has conquered death and sin for the whole world. Sin is no longer counted against the world (2 Cor. 5:19). Henceforth, the Father only views humanity in light of the redeeming work of the Son, born out of the very love of God.

There is also the personal dimension of reconciliation. Christ's death does not automatically achieve salvation for all humanity, but it makes it possible for all to respond in faith. By responding in faith, humanity receives *justification*. Justification means the forgiveness of sin. It is only through faith in Christ that one is justified (Rom. 3:24). No one needs to claim his or her own righteousness before God because each is forgiven and considered righteous in Christ (Rom. 10:3–4). Salvation, then, is the gift of God through Christ by which humanity is reconciled to God and justified by faith.

New Birth

However, to stop at this initial reconciliation through justification is to miss the complete work that God intends for salvation. Salvation is much more than having one's sins forgiven by Christ. Yes, Christ died so that Christians could die—literally—with no fear. But there is more. Christ is both the pattern and the possibility of a metaphorical death. In Romans 6:6–7, Paul states: "We know that our old self was crucified with him in order that the body of sin might be brought to nothing, so that we would no longer be enslaved to sin. For one who has died has been set free from sin" (ESV). Through dying with Christ through faith, a believer becomes "dead to sin." Forgiven of sin, but also *dead to sin*. What does *dead to sin* mean? Paul continues.

"Now if we have died with Christ, we believe that we will also live with him" (6:8, ESV). Human life is ushered into the new creation through new birth. "No longer a slave" of this world, we are reborn and regenerated because Christ has set us "free from the law of sin and death" (Gal. 4:7; Rom. 8:2). To be reborn means more than being dead to sin. To be regenerated means we begin to walk a new life. We begin to walk in step with God's Spirit. We begin to take on the character of Christ. We are *made new*.

We are also *adopted* into the family of God. Although all human beings are children of God in some sense, this belonging is only full actualized in the rebirth of salvation. Just as sin has been forgiven and we have been justified through the death of Christ, we now experience adoption and rebirth; these have their foundation in Jesus's resurrection (1 Peter 1:3). Through his death and resurrection, Jesus Christ claims victory over the power of death and darkness, the ways of the old creation, *and* brings forth new creation in the kingdom of God. Therefore, in Christ, humanity is invited to enter the kingdom and become adopted as children of God—in more than the general sense (1 John 3:1). "The old has passed away" and "the new has come" (2 Cor. 5:17, ESV), both internally as new life and externally as adoption into the family of God; we walk with others who are living anew. As Wesley persistently states in his overall theology and his personal letters to his followers in particular, Christians—forgiven, reborn, and adopted—must now continue to move forward in God's work of salvation by becoming like the Christ who has worked within them.

Participation

Being justified by faith and reborn into the new creation, Scripture tells us that humanity is ascended with Christ, through the Spirit, into the life of God (Eph. 2:4–6). By putting off the sins of the world, humans become "partakers of the divine nature" (2 Peter 1:4, ESV). Through Christ's resurrection and ascension, humanity participates in the Trinitarian life of God (see chapter 4). In other words, we are drawn into the fellowship between the Father and the Son through the power of the Holy Spirit, and in that fellowship our very nature is transformed.

What does it mean to participate in the life of God? This concept seems abstract and mysterious. Once again, Scripture uses a variety of images: transformation "from one degree of glory to another" (2 Cor. 3:18, NRSV); "attaining . . . the fullness of Christ" (Eph. 4:13); sanctification (Rom. 6:19, 22; 1 Thess. 4:3; 2 Thess. 2:13); perfection (Matt 5:48); renewal of mind (Rom. 12:2); "walk[ing] in the light, as he is in the light" (1 John 1:7).

Essentially, when disciples participate in the life of Christ, we become like him. This process by which we are made more Christlike is called *sanctification*. Wesleyans have always asserted that righteousness and holiness are imparted to believers in our day-to-day reality through the sanctifying Spirit of Christ. That is, one is not merely *counted* as righteous (justified), but through sanctification, one actually *becomes* righteous or holy in this life. The goal of holiness occurs when Christians allow the Spirit's work of sanctification to grow so deep that their hearts are filled entirely with love for God and neighbor. Human love is made pure and full as we participate in the love and life of God. This is the goal of Christ's work of salvation. In this sense, salvation in its broader meaning is synonymous with God's sanctifying work throughout the Christian's life.

In light of God's gift in Christ, there is an appropriate human response. Wesley encourages Christians to "let your eye be single; aim still at one thing— holy, loving faith, giving God the whole heart."[5] God does not typically fill with perfect love those who are not vigorously seeking after it.

So why did God become a human in Jesus Christ? To reconcile humanity back to God's self, to open the way for humans to be reborn and adopted as chil-

---

5. Wesley, *Letters*, 4:113.

dren of God's kingdom, and to sanctify humanity, making them more and more like Christ. This is the goal and purpose of human existence. This is salvation.

Discussion Questions

1. Who is Jesus? What did he accomplish in his life, death, resurrection, and ascension? What does the accomplishment of Jesus have to do with our salvation?

2. How does salvation "in Christ" differ from the salvation images of the cultures around you?

3. What are you saved *from*? What are you saved *for*?

4. How should humans respond to the gift of salvation?

Suggestions for Further Reading

Balthasar, Hans Urs von. *Mysterium Paschale: The Mystery of Easter.* San Francisco: Ignatius, 2005.

Green, Joel. *Why Salvation?* Nashville: Abingdon Press, 2014.

Noble, T. A. *Holy Trinity: Holy People: The Theology of Christian Perfecting.* Eugene, OR: Cascade, 2013.

Wesley, John. "The Scripture Way of Salvation." *Sermons II.* Vol. 2 of *The Bicentennial Edition of the Works of John Wesley,* edited by Albert C. Outler. Nashville: Abingdon Press, 1985.

thirteen

WHY IS SANCTIFICATION SO IMPORTANT?

— ∞ —

David McEwan

Have you ever played word association games? (Someone gives you a word and you must quickly respond with another word that you associate with the first one.) It can be a funny—as well as revealing!—game. What word do you associate with *sanctification*?

Sanctification is defined as making a person, place, or object holy, but for many of us it is often seen in terms of all the things we don't do and places we don't go. Many Christians think that, in order to become holy, we are required to actively work at removing those elements of our life that create a barrier between ourselves and God. This practice is presumably best done by obeying the rules and regulations given to us in Scripture so our behavior conforms to God's requirements, emphasizing a life of self-denial and strict discipline. Yet this train of thought binds spirituality to secondary concerns, making holiness synonymous with defined patterns of social correctness, elevating principles over relationships and duty over people. An emphasis on self-denial leads us to value the spiritual over the physical, leading to an unhealthy dualism in which the inner life is regarded as the most important concern.

Love: Holiness Defined

At the heart of John Wesley's theological understanding is the claim that the essential nature of God is love and that this is expressed relationally within the triune Godhead, and then with the creatures God made. A full understanding of sanctification is, therefore, explicitly and necessarily tied to love: "Love is the sum of Christian sanctification: It is the one kind of holiness which is found, only in various degrees, in the believers who are distinguished by St. John into 'little children, young men [and women], and fathers [and mothers].' The difference between one and the other properly lies in the degree of love."[1]

This theological framework affirms that the goal of salvation in Christ is to "'love the Lord thy God with all thy soul, and thy neighbor as thyself.' The Bible declares, 'Love is the fulfilling of the Law,' 'the end of the commandment,' of all the commandments which are contained in the oracles of God."[2] The danger is to think of *love* and *relationship* as empty terms that we can fill with our own content, whereas their character is defined by God's nature and activity, particularly as they are revealed to us in the person and work of Jesus Christ. To love as God loves is to be holy as God is holy—because divine love is absolutely incompatible with selfishness and idolatry. Loving another with integrity means you cannot do, say, or think things that would damage that person *or* yourself. Heart holiness is not primarily about separation from the sinful but a positive engagement with God and the neighbor from a heart of pure love. It is not that beliefs, rituals, and practices are unimportant, but they are clearly subordinate to the primacy of love and relationships.

The evidence that we are not self-deceived about the nature of our love comes from keeping God's commandments—because love rejoices to obey and to do what God desires. Wesley can say very simply that to love as God loves is to be holy as God is holy because to wholeheartedly love God and neighbor is to fulfill all the commandments.

Sanctification: The Experiential Way to Holiness

Encountering the love of God is inherently transformative, and as we embark on a relationship with God, our character and all that flows from it will be increasingly changed into the likeness of Christ. This is the process of sanctification that begins at the experience of our new birth, that then leads to a later moment when God's love entirely fills the heart and expels all that is contrary to love—the moment of *entire sanctification*. Such an experience is still not an end point because our capacity to receive and give love is limitless, as is our capability and opportunity to express that love in words and actions.

Restoring the relationship with God, then, is not just about forgiveness and pardon; it is also about changing our heart's inclination to love the creation above the Creator (idolatry). This misplaced love is a critical issue and lies at the core of the nature of sin (see chapter 9). When we were born again, the change began from inward sinfulness to inward holiness. Our love of the creature began to change into the love of the Creator, the love of the world into the love of God, earthly desires into heavenly desires. Those of us who trust in Christ have found

---

1. Wesley, *Letters*, 4:170.
2. Wesley, Sermon 112, "On Laying the Foundation," in *Sermons III*, vol. 3 of *Works* B, 585.

new life in him, the love of God is poured into our hearts by the Spirit, and there is deliverance from the power of sin.

Wesley believed that, as long as new believers walk in love, which *they may always do*, they have power over both outward and inward sin, even though both Scripture and experience demonstrate that sin remains in the heart. Because the essence of salvation is a restored relationship and Christ is present with the believer, then: "Where the sickness is, there is the physician. Christ indeed cannot *reign* where sin *reigns*; neither will he *dwell* where any sin is *allowed*. But he *is* and *dwells* in the heart of every believer who is fighting against all sin."[3] Wesley strongly believed that the doctrine of the "necessity of sinning"—that is, the more Calvinist belief that we, even as Christians, will always sin continually—is actually destructive of the hope for holy living. If we do not have a confidence in the power of God's grace to deal with the sin within us, then we will always be limiting God's work in our lives.

The work of God needs to go deeper and deeper (what Wesley called the "repentance of believers") as the Holy Spirit uncovers and makes known to us the truth concerning the corruption and deceitfulness of our nature. In all of this we are utterly helpless to change ourselves; only the Lord can change the heart. There should be an increase in love from the first experience of God's redemption until a person is thoroughly convinced of "remaining sin" and trusts God to fill the heart with love, expelling all sin and purifying the heart. This, again, is what Wesley means by entire sanctification. Wesley reminds us that if there is no such change (subsequent to the new-birth experience), if there is no instantaneous deliverance after justification, if there is nothing but a gradual work of God, then we must be content to live with sin until death itself delivers us. Rather, we do need to trust God and God's promises, for what God promises, God will do (1 Thess. 5:23–24).

This idea of entire sanctification of Wesley's is foundational to the Wesleyan-holiness tradition. But to remind us again, Wesley never separates sanctification from love. He emphasizes that, "'Love is the fulfilling of the law.' I believe this love is given in a moment. But about this I contend not. Have this love, and it is enough. For this I will contend till my spirit returns to God."[4] God's Spirit bears witness to this new depth of relationship, along with the outward changes in relationships and conduct.

Perfect Love: Living the Life of Holiness

Love filling the heart can be envisioned in two distinct but interrelated ways. The first involves our capability to love—our inclination to love God and

---

3. Wesley, Sermon 13, "Sin in Believers," in *Sermons I*, vol. 1 of *Works* B, 323.
4. Wesley, "To 'John Smith,'" in *Letters II*, ed. Frank Baker, vol. 26 of *Works* B, 159.

neighbor as we ought. It is the work of the Holy Spirit through sanctification that creates and shapes this inclination as God always intended, rather than it being directed in selfish and idolatrous ways due to our sinfulness. Sanctifying grace empowers our ability to love.

The second element is our capacity to receive and give love. First Corinthians 13:8 tells us that love will never end. This means our capacity for love will continue to expand, both in terms of being filled with the love of the infinite God in an ever increasing measure, and the depths of love that we can then share with the neighbor.

Through the work of the Spirit, our capacity to receive and give love, as well as our inclination, or capability, to share love with both God and neighbor may always increase. This fullness of love Wesley terms *Christian perfection*, and it is clearly defined in terms of our present human condition, not our condition before the fall or after resurrection.

If we are to live in Christian perfection and have strong, healthy relationships that glorify God and form us into Christ's likeness, we will need to embrace God's grace, wisdom, discernment, and guidance. We must be receptive to the work of the Holy Spirit through the body of Christ and the means of grace. Particular cases and particular practices will always need the guidance of the Spirit, both personally and communally. We discern this guidance best by looking to Scripture and the public, long-time interpretation, application, and demonstration of its message. Above all, Wesley said, we must realize that no Scripture passage or teaching of the church can ever overturn the truth that God is love or that God's desire for us all is to live in loving relationships.

Imperfections and Infirmities: The Limits of Sanctification in This Life

For Wesley, our ability to think, evaluate, and judge is compromised by our current bodily existence. Though God's work of salvation in this present life is able to deliver us from the reign of sin in our hearts, it does not bring about a full deliverance from all the *consequences* of personal or social sin, or systemic evil, let alone the devastation wrought on the rest of God's created order. There is clearly an already-not yet tension in Wesley's understanding of Christ's work. We *already* experience a great deliverance from the power of sin, but it is *not yet* a final deliverance, in which all things will be made new. In other words, Wesley clearly limits perfection in this life to love—the love of God received in its fullness and shared by grace with the neighbor.

Wesley writes repeatedly that there is no perfection in knowledge or freedom from ignorance in this life, nor from the mistakes that arise from them. We cannot ever have knowledge that is perfect in extent (though we can be sure of things essential to salvation), and this limitation leads to misjudgments of people and actions, as well as our understanding and application of Scripture.

Even mature Christians deal with the consequences of weak and limited understanding—confusion, inaccuracy, mistakes, false judgments, and wanderings of imagination. These inward or outward imperfections are not of a moral nature and so are not sin because there is no condemnation for things we have no power to choose otherwise.

Likewise, in this life, we are not free from bodily infirmities. The physical nature of the body living in a disordered and corrupted environment makes it liable to weakness, sickness, disorder, pain, and death. These too are amoral. Furthermore, there is no freedom from temptation, since Jesus himself faced this all his earthly life.

Overall, the call to holiness is a real call to live a life of love, through the enabling power of God's sanctifying work in our lives, which continues from new birth to entire sanctification, and on through until our death. We believe in the power of grace and that God's sanctifying work is greater than the power of sin. In the light of our present reality, filled with infirmities and imperfections, it is important to see that holiness and sanctification are not a cure-all for every human need; nevertheless, regarding our inclinations toward holiness and away from sin, we stand in constant need of the merits of Christ's death every moment. Wesley stresses that the whole basis of our restored relationship with God, and our renewal in the image of Christ, is God's grace and never our own achievement.

A sanctified life is essentially the indwelling presence of the triune God—the Father, Son, and Holy Spirit—and their pure love filling the heart, expelling all that is contrary to God's character in us. This love is then to be fully and freely returned to God in an ever deepening relationship; this love then spills over and embraces all neighbors and their welfare. It is this pure love that molds and shapes our nature into the very likeness of Christ, in spite of the current limitations of our bodily existence.

Discussion Questions

1. Why do you think so many prefer to think of holiness and sanctification in terms of keeping rules and regulations?

2. How can we love someone without actually liking him or her? What difference would this make for difficult relationships in the church or community?

3. Why do we tend to link duty and obedience more easily than love and obedience?

4. How do we tell the difference between sin and infirmity? What happens to our understanding of sanctification if we see them as being essentially the same?

Suggestions for Further Reading

Leclerc, Diane. *Discovering Christian Holiness: The Heart of Wesleyan-Holiness Theology*. Kansas City: Beacon Hill Press of Kansas City, 2010.

Noble, T. A. *Holy Trinity: Holy People: The Historic Doctrine of Christian Perfecting*. Eugene, OR: Cascade Books, 2013.

Sanders, Fred. *Wesley on the Christian Life: The Heart Renewed in Love*. Wheaton, IL: Crossway, 2013.

fourteen
WHAT MAKES ETHICS CHRISTIAN?

——∞∞∞——

Gift Mtukwa

Christian ethics are where the rubber meets the road. Our theological beliefs are tested by the way we live our lives. For the most part, the people we encounter don't care much about our beliefs—but they certainly care about our actions, since our actions affect them. Our beliefs are only important as they influence our actions. Christian ethics in the Wesleyan perspective affirm that our beliefs make a difference in how we live our lives. Holiness, as our distinctive doctrine, is about living a markedly different kind of life.

The word *ethics* is defined here as "the study of how to make morally good and right decisions from Christian perspective," or, as Roger Crook says, "critical evaluation of human conduct from a Christian perspective."[1] The study of ethics is by definition concerned about the process or rationale we use to arrive at moral judgments. For Christians, this process is extremely important since we are constantly faced with moral dilemmas that require us to use the Christian faith to assess which of our alternatives is the Christian decision.

First and foremost, Scripture is important in formulating a Wesleyan ethic. Scripture ought to be consulted first, and, according to John Wesley, "the whole tenor of Scripture"[2] ought to be consulted. However, Scripture has to be read properly in order to provide proper guidance for moral behavior, for even Scripture can be used to justify immoral behavior. In the words of H. Ray Dunning, "We must beware of using biblical characters as comprehensive models for ethical behavior. Only Jesus can serve as such an ethical model; all others, even

---

1. Roger Crook, *An Introduction to Christian Ethics* (Englewood Cliffs, NJ: Prentice Hall, 1990), 1.
2. See Wesley, "Free Grace," in *Works*, 7:379–80.

the best, must be critically evaluated."[3] Just as in the doing of Wesleyan theology, Scripture does not function alone (see chapter 3), so can other supporting sources of authority in moral judgment be used as well.

Besides following Scripture in developing a Christian ethic, and espousing ethical conduct, John Wesley talks about why God raised the people called Methodists specifically: "To reform the nation; particularly the church, and to spread scriptural holiness across the land."[4] It is clear in what we might call the mission statement of Methodism that Wesley's goal is to change society. It is interesting that "to reform the nation" comes even before the call to "reform the church." For Wesley, the two are an integral part of being the people of God. However, Wesley's children have focused more on spreading scriptural holiness, at times, at the expense of reforming the nation. In Wesley's thought, the two need to go together, and it would be unthinkable to have one without the other. Inward holiness and social holiness, as Wesley calls it, are inseparable. Wesley would question the legitimacy of any testimony to living the holy life if that person did not act in specific ways to impact the people and change the surrounding society.

Wesleyan Ethics: Grounded in the *Imago Dei*

Wesleyan ethics are grounded in the fact that humanity is created in the image of God. All that can be said about humanity stems from the fact that we were first made in God's image; in Wesleyan interpretation, the image refers to the capacity for loving relationships, which certainly has an ethical dimension. The aspect that concerns us here is what Wesley called the moral image of God, in which humanity is characterized by original holiness or wholeness. In this holiness, Adam and Eve's relationships are *functional*—that is, their relationship with God, with each other, with the earth, and even within themselves. H. Ray Dunning talks about the image of God in terms of freedoms: freedom for God, freedom for the other, freedom from the world (or for the earth), and freedom from self-domination,[5] or self-destruction. The fall into sin disrupts these relationships. God has not left us in that quagmire, but through grace—commonly called prevenient grace—God is in some way redeeming humanity from its destructive situation and wooing it back into holy or whole relationships. This is the reason the writers of *Upward Call* say, "Spiritual Formation (ethics) must

---

3. H. Ray Dunning, *Christian Ethics in Wesleyan Perspective: Reflecting the Divine Image* (Downers Grove, IL: InterVarsity Press, 1998), 20.

4. Wesley, "Minutes of Several Conversations," Q. 3, in *Works*, 8:299.

5. H. Ray Dunning, *Grace, Faith, and Holiness* (Kansas City: Beacon Hill Press of Kansas City, 1988), 478–98.

recognize that God's design has been seriously frustrated by sin."[6] In ethical terminology, the immoral is by definition essentially sin—that which disrupts and destroys relationships. This is a strong statement. According to Leon Hynson, it is only because of prevenient grace that "everyone is capable of moral action, and is morally responsible. Morality is an intimate expression and consequence of grace."[7] Without prevenient grace, humanity would only be capable of sin.

In the context of prevenient grace, what we might refer to as *conscience* can also be discussed. According to John Wesley, there is no person who is in a state of nature, as are Adam and Eve before the fall; the fall actually invokes God's compassion (rather than pure wrath), and prevenient grace is given to humanity from that time on; therefore, no one is devoid of the grace of God.[8] From this perspective, any good that a person does is in fact the result of the grace of God at work in each and every individual's life. As Dunning says, in this way Christian ethics "is an extension of the [original] creation ethic toward the achievement of full personhood. . . . In the fullest religious sense it is an ethic that enhances rather than perverts the humanity of [persons]."[9] In this sense, Wesleyans are not taken aback by those who live moral lives and yet are not believers. They are simply paying attention to the "light which 'enlightens every man that cometh into the world,'" to use Wesley's words.[10]

Wesleyan Ethics: Founded on Salvation in Christ

But even in light of God's prevenient grace, God's desire for humanity is ultimately frustrated. It is really the *salvation* of Christ as new birth that provides the real impetus for living ethical lives. The all-encompassing salvation we have in Christ deals effectively with the sin problem. Since sin affects us at the core of our being, salvation reverses the effects of sin as relationships are restored.[11] Wesley defines salvation thus: "By salvation I mean, not barely, deliverance from hell, or going to heaven, but a present deliverance from sin, a restoration of the soul to its primitive health, its original purity; a recovery of the divine nature; the renewal of our souls after the image of God in the righteousness and true holiness, in justice, mercy, truth. This implies all holy and heavenly tempers, and by consequence all holiness of conversation."[12] There is no doubt that this un-

---

6. Wesley D. Tracy et al., *Upward Call: Spiritual Formation and the Holy Life* (Kansas City: Beacon Hill Press of Kansas City, 1994), 26.

7. Leon O. Hynson, *To Reform the Nation: Theological Foundations of Wesley's Ethics* (Grand Rapids: Francis Asbury Press, 1984), 33.

8. Wesley, "Working Out Our Own Salvation," in *Works*, 6:512.

9. Dunning, *Grace, Faith, and Holiness*, 499.

10. Wesley, "Predestination Calmly Considered," in *Works*, 10:229-30.

11. The fourfold relationships of God, others, earth, and self.

12. Maddox, *Responsible Grace*, 145.

derstanding of salvation is laden with ethical overtones. Our relationships—once tainted by sin—are restored, and we are able to stand before God, others, the environment, and ourselves with integrity. For Wesley, salvation means a change of lifestyle, attitude, and temper.

In Protestant fashion, this salvation is by grace through faith. Christian ethics are grace enabled, since the whole of the Christian life from beginning to end is grace enabled. It is by grace not only to *know* the right thing but also to *do* the right thing. In this way, Christian ethics are only for the redeemed people of God, for without grace, the ethical requirements of Jesus are indeed insurmountable; however, with grace they are an "impossible possibility" (to use Reinhold Niebuhr's phrase).[13]

Wesleyan Ethics: The Call to Holy Living

The ability to live out Christian ethics only comes through being transformed within. It is none other than being renewed in the image of God. This transformation and renewal come through God's sanctifying work and result in being filled to overflowing with God's love. Love is a crucial part of a Wesleyan theology of ethics. Once sin has been dealt with, we are free to love God and neighbor with all our heart, soul, and mind. For Wesley, the result of having the love of God shed abroad in our hearts is that it expels "the love of the world, together with pride, anger, self-will, and every other evil temper, changing the earthly, sensual, devilish mind, into 'the mind which was in Christ Jesus.'"[14] This love is nothing but perfect love, which is "love excluding sin; love filling the heart, taking up the whole capacity of the soul."[15]

Hynson captures the relationship between love and ethics when he asserts, "It is the new life of love that permeates our affections, will, and intellect, shaping relationships with others, influencing decisions, and forging thought patterns that are in conformity to the mind of Jesus Christ. Love sets the tone for action, helps set Christian priorities, and inspires to the realization of the Christian's calling."[16] Again, Wesleyan theology does not have a place for withdrawal from the world to seek personal holiness. One is called not only to love those in the church but also the ungodly. Wesley was right to note that there is "no holiness but social holiness."[17]

---

13. Reinhold Niebuhr, *An Interpretation of Christian Ethics* (New York: Charles Scribner's Sons, 1935), 19.

14. Wesley, "The Scripture Way of Salvation," in *Works*, 6:45.

15. Ibid., 46.

16. Hynson, *To Reform the Nation*, 95–96.

17. Wesley, "List of Poetical Works," in *Works*, 14:321.

Many of the virtues (fruits of the Spirit) of the Christian faith are tested in the community. One can only know they are kind if that kindness is tested by others in the community. In the sermon "Scripture Way of Salvation," Wesley talks about two essential types of good works. One is "works of piety," which entails prayer, participating in the Lord's Table, Scripture reading, fasting, and so on. Second is the "works of mercy," such as ministering to the souls of men and women in prison, the sick, and all those at the mercy of society. According Hynson, this is Wesley's way of balancing between personal and social concerns.[18]

Wesleyan Ethics: Examples

Many of Wesley's works of mercy are tied to the proper use of money. His attitude toward money is demonstrated when he says, "In the hands of his children, it is food for the hungry, drink for the thirsty, raiment for the naked: it gives to the traveler and the stranger where to lay his head. By it may supply the place of an husband to the widow, and of a father to the fatherless, defense for the oppressed, a means of health to the sick, of ease to them that are in pain; it may be as eyes to the blind, as feet to the lame."[19] Wesley gives three further pieces of advice: "Gain all you can, save all you can, and give all you can." This short encouragement summarizes Wesley's approach to money. Christians are to use their abilities to acquire wealth, provided they don't hurt themselves—body and soul, or sell anything that would hurt the neighbor.[20] Wesley seems to have a message applicable to some of today's companies when he says, "Who purposely lengthens the pain or diseases which they are able to remove speedily? Who protracts the cure of their patient's body, in order to plunder his substance?"[21] He implies that this will result in judgment from God. All this, for Wesley, is a failure to love one's neighbor as oneself.

For Wesley "save all you can" is not advice to stash money in a chest or a bank but, rather, not to "throw it away in idle expenses,"[22] which he equates to throwing it in the sea. Wesley draws personal ethics from this idea when he says, "Expend no part of it merely to gratify the desires of the flesh, the desire of the eye, or the pride of life."[23] To the consumerism of our day and age, Wesley might say, "Despise delicacy and variety and be content with what plain nature requires."[24]

18. Hynson, *To Reform the Nation*, 105.
19. Wesley, "The Use of Money," in *Works*, 6:126.
20. Ibid., 128.
21. Ibid., 129.
22. Ibid., 131.
23. Ibid.
24. Ibid.

Gaining and saving all that one can is not enough; one needs also to give all one can. Giving has a hierarchy for Wesley; Christians begin by meeting their own needs, the needs of their families, those of the household of faith, and the rest of all persons.[25] In all this the principle is, "Render unto God not a tenth, not a third, not half, but all that is God's."[26] Wesley himself is an example of stewardship in that he did not increase his expenses when his income grew; rather, that added income meant more money to give to those in need.

The Holiness Movement of the nineteenth and twentieth centuries seems to have put into practice Wesley's moral vision. The movement on the social side placed emphasis on abolition of slavery, women's rights, temperance, child welfare, and the care of the poor, the sick, and the imprisoned.[27] Rodney L. Reed says of the holiness people that "their social ethics arose out of their personal piety and much of the personal ethics was seen to have clear social ramifications."[28] This specific statement clearly captures what Hynson says of the Wesleyan ethic more generally: "The ethic of holiness is an ethic of the cross, a cruciform ethics wherein the divine and human intersect and unite."[29] Such an ethic is more than relevant today, as it has been in our past.

Discussion Questions

1. To what extent should Wesleyans follow Wesley's spending habits? Critique today's materialism using Wesley's approach to money.

2. How are the social ethics of the Wesleyan-holiness tradition in the past related to issues today, such as human trafficking?

3. How do we explain goodness in non-Christians? How does Christ make our ethics complete?

Suggestions for Further Reading

Crook, Roger H. *An Introduction to Christian Ethics.* Englewood Cliffs, NJ: Prentice Hall, 1990.

Dunning, H. Ray. *Christian Ethics in Wesleyan Perspective: Reflecting the Divine Image.* Downers Grove, IL: InterVarsity Press, 1998.

Hynson, Leon O. *To Reform the Nation: Theological Foundations of Wesley's Ethics.* Grand Rapids: Francis Asbury Press, 1984.

---

25. Ibid., 134.

26. Ibid., 135.

27. Rodney L. Reed, *Holy with Integrity: The Unity of Personal and Social Ethics in the Holiness Movement, 1880-1910* (Salem, OH: Schmul Publishing Company, 2002), 8.

28. Reed, *Holy with Integrity,* 13.

29. Hynson, *To Reform the Nation,* 102.

Maddox, Randy L. *Responsible Grace: John Wesley's Practical Theology.* Nashville: Kingswood, 1994.

Reed, Rodney L. *Holy with Integrity: The Unity of Personal and Social Ethics in the Holiness Movement, 1880–1910.* Salem, OH: Schmul Publishing Company, 2002.

Tracy, Wesley D., et al. *Upward Call: Spiritual Formation and the Holy Life.* Kansas City: Beacon Hill Press of Kansas City, 1994.

fifteen
HOW DO WE GROW SPIRITUALLY?

———∞∞∞———

Mark A. Maddix

One of the primary goals of Christians is to grow spiritually, to become more and more like Christ. In order to grow spiritually, Christians participate in a variety of disciplines and practices. Many of these practices are learned informally while others are intentionally developed. Historically, Christians have embraced a variety of practices in order to experience God, some of which continue to inform Christian life and practice today. However, many Christians struggle to know how to grow spiritually. They struggle with developing consistent practices because of a limited and narrow understanding of what is available. Many Christians, even Wesleyans, are unaware of their rich heritage and its witness of transforming persons and society.

Wesleyan theology is an experiential and practiced theology. John Wesley was a pastor who worked out his theology through his ministry. He did not separate what he believed about God from what he did in ministry. His theology informed his practice, and his practices shaped his theology. This *praxis* approach (theology and practice) is at the heart of the Wesleyan movement. Wesleyan theology is a *lived* theology. The primary goal of the Wesleyan movement is the transformation of the human person into the likeness of Jesus Christ, which includes cooperation between humans and God's transforming grace. This description is synonymous with the familiar word *sanctification*. This goal of transformation is reflected in Galatians 4:19: "My dear children, for whom I am again in the pains of childbirth until Christ is *formed* in you" (emphasis added). Paul uses the word *morphoō* (form), closely related to *metamorphoō* (transform)—and it refers to a metamorphosis of the essential nature, not mere outward form. Paul is praying that the inward nature of the Galatian believers would become so like Christ that one could say Christ has been *formed* in them. They would be more like Christ in his humanity—not divine themselves, but they would have real,

Christlike character and behavior.[1] Spiritual growth, then, is the outworking of the grace of God in the changed hearts and actions of human beings.

A Wesleyan approach to spiritual formation (progressive sanctification) begins through God's grace toward us; we are called to respond and participate with God in our formation. A Wesleyan view of spiritual formation can be summed up with the following definition: "a process of being transformed into Christlikeness, through communal practices and participation in the 'means of grace,' while giving attention to the care of self, which is demonstrated in loving others and being actively engaged in God's redemption of all of creation."[2]

Means of Grace

We cannot conform *ourselves* to the image of Christ, but God conforms and transforms us by the power of the Spirit. However, a Wesleyan theology of grace focuses on cooperation between God and humans. God and human persons act synergistically (dynamically together). God's transforming grace freely flows to those who actively receive it, and to receive grace you must be an active participant. In other words, when you engage in spiritual formational practices, you are being opened to receive grace from God. If you don't engage in spiritual formational practices, you are limiting the opportunities for yourself to grow spiritually and to receive God's grace. The old adage is true: *Practice makes us perfect.* The more we practice our faith, the more we grow spiritually. These practices become habits that develop into virtues. For example, a compassionate person is compassionate because he or she has practiced compassion on a regular basis; outward actions become inward attitudes, and inward attitudes lead to outward actions. In the same way as we engage in regular spiritual practices, our lives are being conformed and transformed into the image and likeness of Christ.

John Wesley calls these practices the "means of grace." In his sermon "The Means of Grace," he states, "By means of grace I understand outward signs, words, or actions, ordained by God, and appointed for this end, to be ordinary channels whereby God might convey to [people] [prevenient], justifying and sanctifying grace."[3] Wesley uses the word *means* with the word *ordinance* on occasion as an indicator that this participation is expected by God. While the means of grace themselves have no salvific worth, they are channels by which the Holy Spirit works in our hearts.

---

1. Tracy et al., *Upward Call*, 9.
2. This definition was developed by Mark A. Maddix and is fleshed out in his chapter "Living the Life: Spiritual Formation Defined" in *Spiritual Formation: A Wesleyan Paradigm*, ed. Diane Leclerc and Mark A. Maddix (Kansas City: Beacon Hill Press of Kansas City, 2011), 9–17.
3. Wesley, Sermon 16, "The Means of Grace," in *Sermons I*, vol. 1 of *Works* B, 381.

Wesley divides the means of grace into three divisions: instituted, prudential, and general (see chart 1). The instituted means of grace are practices that Christ asks his disciples to do and model. They include prayer, searching the Scriptures, participating in the Lord's Supper (Eucharist), fasting, and Christian conferencing (small groups). The prudential means of grace are practices that are wise and beneficial to do. They include obeying Christ, special prayer meetings, visiting the sick, doing all the good we can to all the people we can, and reading from the devotional classics of the rich tradition of two thousand years of Christianity. The prudential means of grace are designed to meet the person at his or her point of need—thus, they are adaptable to a person's particular historical situation or context. The general means of grace include watching, denying ourselves, taking up our crosses daily, and exercising the presence of God.

Chart 1: Means of Grace Domains

Instituted	Prudential	General
The means that Christ asks his disciples to do or model. • Praying • Searching Scripture • Lord's Supper • Fasting • Christian Conferencing (Small Groups)	The means that are wise and beneficial to do. • Obedience to Christ • Prayer Meetings • Visiting the Sick • Doing Good to All People • Reading Christian Classics	The means that maintain and foster our relationship with God. • Watching • Denying Ourselves • Taking up the Cross Daily • Exercising the Presence of God

Wesley doesn't confine God's grace just to these practices. Because he understands grace to be God's loving, uncreated presence, he believes many other activities can qualify as means of grace. It is an interesting question what we might add to Wesley's list today. Wesley believes that, through participation in the means of grace, a person can be made aware of God's pardoning and the empowering presence of Christ on a regular basis.

Wesley's ideas here have sometimes been called therapeutic. By that, we mean that Wesley often talks about sin as disease and holiness as healing. Thus, the means of grace provide healing for the soul, or character. Wesley's therapeutic focus is evident in his invitation for his people to meditate regularly on the affirmation that Christ "sealed his love with sacraments of grace, to breed and nourish up in us the life of love."[4] Thus, all who need further empowering by God's grace should faithfully participate in the instituted means of grace.

Instituted Means of Grace (Works of Piety)

By *instituted means of grace*, we mean that Christ himself instructs or even commands his disciples to follow certain spiritual practices. Wesley believes people should use these practices "with a constant eye" toward the renewal of their souls in "righteousness and true holiness."[5] He believes these practices will expose persons to, and ultimately shape persons into, the character of God.

Prayer

One of the bedrocks of spiritual formation is prayer and Scripture reading. Many Christians recognize that conversation with God in prayer and reading Scripture results in spiritual food and nourishment. Prayer is a practice that nurtures the heart and soul of the believer.

Wesley encourages Christians to pray on a regular basis, following his revised Book of Common Prayer (BCP) for prayer and worship called *The Sunday Service of the Methodists in North America*.[6] He published *Devotions for Every Day in the Week* in order to guide and encourage daily prayer among his readers. He followed the daily offices developed by the Anglican church that include prayer, psalms, collects, and hymns. Wesley believes that at the heart of growing spiritually is engaging in the rhythm of praying without ceasing.

For Christians today, certainly prayer is bringing our requests to God; but prayer can take a variety of forms, such as meditation, silence, and active listening. There is a growing interest among Christians to engage in prayer activities that nurture their souls and connect them with God. Prayer is transformative in both private and church contexts.

Searching the Scriptures

Reading and interpreting the Bible, or searching the Scriptures, is another significant practice that helps Christians grow spiritually. As discussed in chapters 2 and 3, Wesleyans read Scripture as *formation* instead of just *information*. Scripture was given to the church as a means of forming Christians into faithful disciples. Searching the Scriptures implies a meditative reading where the Holy Spirit inspires our hearts. If prayer is our breath, Scripture is our food. We need food in order to survive and thrive.

---

4. Maddox, *Responsible Grace,* 200.

5. Wesley, Sermon 24, "Sermon on the Mount, IV," in *Sermons I,* vol. 1 of *Works* B, 545.

6. John Wesley, *John Wesley's Prayer Book: The Sunday Service of the Methodists in North America,* ed. James F. White (Cleveland: OSL Publications, 1991).

Wesley did not create a novel method of Bible study, but he seems to have observed the ancient practice of *lectio divina* (sacred readings), developed in the fifth century by Benedict of Nursia. The practice is a slow, contemplative praying of the Scriptures that enables Scripture to become a means of communion with God. *Lectio divina* is a process of scriptural encounter that includes a series of prayer dynamics that move the reader to a deep level of engagement with the chosen text and with the Spirit who enlivens the text. The movements include silence, readings, praying, contemplation, and compassion.[7] While this practice can be pursued alone, when done in a small group setting, insights and inspiration offer an additional dimension to the practice. Today Christians and faith communities are regaining the significance of this ancient practice as a means to make Bible reading exciting and engaging once again.

Lord's Supper (Eucharist)

John Wesley places a high value on the Lord's Supper in worship. He exhorts Methodists to practice "constant communion."[8] Wesley generally took Communion every four or five days. He believes it is the highest point of Methodist worship and an opportunity to experience and commune with Christ. He believes that, through Communion, persons experience the very presence of Christ.

Wesley doesn't hold to the Roman Catholic view of *transubstantiation* (the bread and wine actually become the body and blood of Christ), but he does believe that Christ is uniquely present. Since Christ is present, everyone is invited to participate, anyone seeking the grace of God. Christ is present spiritually and immediately, interacting with the recipient to give transforming grace. Wesley believes that, through participation in Communion, a person can receive forgiveness and reconciliation through an obedient response to God's grace. Wesley desired to see Methodists and all Christians to take Communion regularly as an essential means of grace so it would result in holiness of heart and life.

Communion is soul food. It nourishes the soul. It is transformative for those who are called and drawn toward holiness and for those who are being sanctified. It is for those who desire to grow in God's grace and want to deepen their love for God and neighbor. Communion is a sacrament that serves not only to preserve and sustain but also to advance progress and growth in faith and holiness. Communion as an act is a personal and communal reminder of Christ's suffering love, as well as a direct activity of the Holy Spirit that provides an immediate way of participating in the ongoing, transforming grace of God.

---

7. Doug Hardy, "Lectio Divina: A Practice for Reconnecting to God's Word," *Preacher's Magazine: A Preaching Resource in the Wesleyan Tradition* (Lent/Easter 2009): 38–41.

8. See Wesley, Sermon 101, "The Duty of Constant Communion," in *Sermons I*, vol. 1 of *Works* B, 427–39.

Many Wesleyan-holiness congregations follow Wesley's practice of Communion often in worship. They recognize that Communion signifies the very meal that sustains and heals the local church. It transforms the entire church not simply as an individual expression of personal piety but as the metaphorical body of Christ, for which the physical body of Christ was sacrificed. Christians recognize that as they breathe in through participation in Word and Table, they are healed, empowered, and equipped to breathe out in God's mission in the world. Communion is one of the most powerful and transformative aspects of Christian worship that helps people grow spiritually.

Fasting

Fasting is an ancient practice that focuses on denying oneself of food or other things in one's life on which one is highly dependent. Wesley was known for fasting from food several days a week, and he encouraged Methodists to fast on Fridays. The American Methodist Church made Friday a day of fasting. Wesley considered it "deplorable" that many Methodists neglected fasting, and his journals are full of his own commitment to fasting. Many Christians today fast a meal on a regular basis and give the money to the needy. Others even provide a technology fast or Sabbath one day a week as part of their spiritual practices. One of the main purposes of fasting is to increase our awareness of our dependence on God.

Christian Conferencing

The next instituted means of grace refers to Christian conferencing, which could include such things as District or General Assemblies that can follow Wesley's understanding of the intentional conversation and consensus of a side group of people, on practical or theological issues. But most often today it refers to the beneficial nature of small groups. As Christians speak about God together, grace is poured out upon the participants. This is why it is important to have a small group of people with whom you meet on a regular basis to tell your story, to talk about your spiritual life, and to learn together. Christian conversation is an intentional, diligent act. It is an act of love as we share our faith and live together in the very presence of the Holy Spirit. The community of believers is intended to be means of mutual support, encouragement, and strength.

One of the most significant avenues that fosters spiritual growth is small groups. John Wesley's group formation provided a context for spiritual growth and development for Methodists. Some argue that his small group formation revolutionized early Methodism and that Wesley is the father of the modern small group concept.[9] Wesley employed a methodical approach to spiritual for-

---

9. David Hunsicker, "John Wesley: Father of Today's Small Groups," *Wesleyan Theological Journal* 31, no. 1 (Spring 1996): 210.

mation that focused on assisting participants to grow in holiness of heart and life. D. Michael Henderson suggests that Wesley's interlocking groups included a hierarchy of instruction for each group, tailored to a specific function. Henderson distinguishes each group as society, class, or band with a specific educational mode.[10] The societies focused primarily on cognitive development, teaching Methodist tenets and doctrine; classes focused on changing and transforming human behavior; and bands focused on growing in holiness and purity of intention. Wesley's group formation incorporated Scripture as central to the small group process. In societies Scripture was read, interpreted, and preached as a normal aspect of meetings. In classes and bands, Scripture was employed as a formative aspect in shaping behavior and holy living.

The class meetings were the most influential in providing spiritual growth and accountability. They were small groups of ten to twelve people who were required to bare their souls and confess sin. The meetings included the leader stating the condition of his or her spiritual life, sharing honestly about failures, sins, temptations, or inner battles. The participants were asked a series of questions including whether they had committed sin that week. Small groups like this are needed in our lives to provide personal and spiritual accountability as we seek holiness of heart and life.

Prudential Means of Grace (Works of Mercy)

The instituted means of grace focus on personal piety while the prudential means of grace focus on works of mercy. The term *prudential* (literally, wise) comes from the emerging belief by the church that inward holiness leads to outward holiness. The prudential means of grace are the primary ways we express our love for neighbor.

In order to grow spiritually, we are to obey God's commandments. When we obey God's commandments we open channels of grace in our lives. When we are disobedient, we block those channels and do not receive grace and are not able to give grace to others. It is through repentance that these channels are reopened for us to receive grace. Wesley placed a strong emphasis on obedience to God's commandments as an important avenue for spiritual growth.

To grow spiritually means following the conviction to "do no harm," which means never to consciously do anything we know would damage someone else. We make this commitment to respect and value others in our personal conduct and in our working contexts. We are to do all the good we can in all the places we can. It means we are to replace evil with good. This includes caring for others and all living things.

---

10. David Michael Henderson, *John Wesley's Class Meeting: A Model of Making Disciples* (Nappanee, IN: Evangel, 1997), 83.

Wesley practiced visiting the sick on a regular basis. He is known for his works of mercy and compassion toward the poor and outcast. He recognized the importance of healing and liberating persons from oppression. Wesley understood that holiness of heart and life was an ongoing goal to be lived out each day. As they sought to live holy lives they were transformed within, but they were also engaged in changing and transforming the world. They participated in the means of grace in order to be a means of grace to others. In other words, growing spiritually was not for them only but for the sake of others and the world. As Christians engage in acts of mercy, compassion, and caring for the poor and oppressed, they grow spiritually and live out God's mission in the world.[11]

General Means of Grace

A person can perhaps practice the instituted and prudential means of grace and just go through the motions without growing spiritually. However, the general means of grace, which require searching, self-examination, and daily reflection on one's attitude and motivations, cause constant attention to God. Such practices as self-denial, watching, and cross-bearing are expressions of conforming to God's will.[12] The denial of sinful thoughts and actions, and self-indulgence, separate us from God. Self-denial is connected with cross-bearing, which is the result of inward transformation. Wesley believed we can grow closer to God when distractions are willingly set aside. In a world that is focused on instant gratification and consumerism, self-denial becomes a challenge for many Christians. Self-denial can help us refocus our attention, devotion, and dependence on God.

We can grow spiritually as we take up our cross by enduring hardships and suffering, and by doing things that go against our natural inclinations. Such acts as feeding the poor, visiting the prisoner, or taking care of widows and orphans go against our natural inclinations.

Christians can grow spiritually by exercising the presence of God by communing with God in all we do. Brother Lawrence helped us understand that we can be aware of God's presence in the midst of washing dishes or any daily activity. If we affirm that it is the very presence of God in our lives that defines spirituality and aids Christian growth, then *practicing* that God is with us is just as important as *trusting* that God is with us.

---

11. See Mark A. Maddix and Jay R. Akkerman, *Missional Discipleship: Partners in God's Redemptive Mission* (Kansas City: Beacon Hill Press of Kansas City, 2013), for a more complete understanding of the role compassion plays in our spiritual formation.

12. Andrew C. Thompson, "The General Means of Grace," *Methodist History* 51:4 (July 2013): 251–52.

Communal Practice: The Church

For Christians to grow spiritually, they must participate in the means of grace. The means of grace encompass both individual and communal practices. One of the most important aspects of Wesleyan spirituality is the church (covered in greater detail in chapters 16 and 17). Spiritual growth takes place through fellowship with other believers, communal worship, and missionary service. Wesley believed religion was social and that personal holiness includes social holiness. His focus on the relational aspects of holiness was about fellowship, or *koinonia*. He recognized that our faith is shaped and formed best in community. The practice of community continues to be a challenge for many Christians in the West who view faith primarily as individualistic and personal; but being Christian means to live in community. If Christians want to grow spiritually, they are to participate in a local church on a regular basis and gather around Word and Table as part of worship.

How do we grow spiritually? What does Wesleyan spirituality look like? Our rich Wesleyan heritage provides a theological canvas for us to see how persons have grown spiritually in the past and how participation in the means of grace can help present and future generations experience the transforming grace of God. As Christians participate in the means of grace, both individually and corporately, they will open up opportunities for themselves to receive grace and become more like Christ.

Discussion Questions

1. What spiritual formational practices are you currently practicing?

2. Based on your understanding of the means of grace, what practices do you need to incorporate in your life?

3. In what ways has being involved in a small group or Bible study that provides accountability helped you grow spiritually?

4. In what ways can you incorporate Bible reading in your spiritual life, including such practices as *lectio divina*?

5. In what ways are you engaged in acts of mercy and compassion? How does this practice help you grow spiritually?

Suggestions for Further Reading

Calhoun, Adele Ahlberg. *Spiritual Disciplines Handbook: Practices That Transform Us*. Downers Grove, IL: InterVarsity Press, 2005.

Jones, Tony. *The Sacred Way: Spiritual Practices for Everyday Life*. Grand Rapids: Zondervan, 2005.

Leclerc, Diane and Mark A. Maddix, eds. *Spiritual Formation: A Wesleyan Paradigm*. Kansas City: Beacon Hill Press of Kansas City, 2011.

Mulholland, M. Robert, Jr. *Invitation to a Journey: A Road Map for Spiritual Formation*. Downers Grove, IL: InterVarsity Press, 1993.

Smith, James Bryan. *A Spiritual Formation Workbook*, rev. ed. San Francisco: HarperOne, 2007.

Thompson, Marjorie J. *Soul Feast: An Invitation to the Christian Spiritual Life*. Louisville: Westminster John Knox Press, 1995.

Tracy, Wesley E., et al. *The Upward Call: Spiritual Formation and Holy Living*. Kansas City: Beacon Hill Press of Kansas City, 1993.

Wilhoit, James C. *Spiritual Formation as if the Church Mattered*. Grand Rapids: Baker Books, 2008.

PART 5

The Church's Meaning, Purpose, and Hope

sixteen

WHAT IS THE CHURCH?

————— ∞ —————

Montague R. Williams

The Nicene Creed announces that the church is "one, holy, catholic, and apostolic." But how can we say and believe this when Christians sense division among one another, recognize sin in their own lives, quarrel over differing beliefs, and do not always bear faithful witness to the gospel of Jesus Christ? This mode of inquiry is central to the theological study of the church, but the complexity of the question and the fact that John Wesley's own discussion of the church is minimal has made the discernment of a Wesleyan ecclesiology a difficult task. Wesleyans, however, do adhere to these creedal statements about the church.

The Church's Oneness

The church's oneness derives from the oneness of God as Father, Son, and Holy Spirit. The church is called together by the Holy Spirit to confess the Lordship of Jesus Christ as the covenanted people of God in the world.[1] As seen in this dynamic interplay of the three Persons of the Trinity, the existence and life of the church rely on the triune existence and life of God. The church is drawn by the Spirit into relation with the triune God and is sent into the world as a reflection of the Trinity's perfect community that maintains an interdependence of unity amidst distinction.[2]

The church is not merely the collection of Christians from across the globe and church history; the church is the *one* body of Christ. It is important to recognize that the term *body* does refer to Christ's body and not simply a large

---

1. "Article XI," in *Manual: Church of the Nazarene: 2013-2017* (Kansas City: Nazarene Publishing House, 2013), 34.

2. See John 17:4–6; also see T. A. Noble, *Holy Trinity: Holy People: The Historic Doctrine of Christian Perfecting* (Eugene, OR: Cascade Books, 2013).

mass, as in a body of water or even a body of believers. The very Holy Spirit who descended on Jesus Christ to guide and sustain him through his ministry of life, death, and resurrection is the same Holy Spirit who has descended into the world to create, inspire, and sustain the church as the one body of Christ.[3]

The problem is that the church is not always experienced as *one*. In fact, various theologians and traditions have made attempts to make sense of this discrepancy. Historical theologian Alister McGrath categorizes these attempts into four approaches.[4] The imperialist approach solves the problem of disunity by identifying one tradition within Christianity as the true church and every other group as failed attempts at being church. The undergirding presupposition here is that observers should be able to rely on empirical evidence—such as leadership structure and decision-making procedures—to determine what the true church is.

The second approach solves the problem of disunity by making a distinction between a visible church and an invisible church. The visible church would be the church we experience, and the invisible church would be either an ideal church currently existing in an unseen realm or the predestined collection of heaven-bound people.

A third and related approach is the eschatological approach, which suggests that the oneness of the church will be fulfilled after the return of Christ and cannot be realized until then. We must wait for the culmination of things to truly see the church.

Finally, the biological approach solves the issue of disunity by viewing the church through the lens of a family tree. It focuses on the development and organic connections of denominations and movements throughout church history.

While each of these approaches offer a way forward, and the latter two come close to a Wesleyan perspective, none of them fully reflects Wesleyan theology. Wesleyans do not identify their tradition or denominations as the true church over other Christian groups. Wesleyans recognize that Christ's real humanity renders human bodies too meaningful in God's relation to the world to rely on an invisible church. Wesleyans do believe that the eschatological reign of God is the fulfillment of God's hope for humanity and all creation. However, Wesleyans also believe it is possible for God's kingdom to come now and God's will to be done "on earth as it is in heaven" (Matt. 6:10).[5]

Finally, Wesleyan theology does appreciate the way different Christian denominations and movements uniquely contribute to the broader Christian family as found in the biological approach, but this does not address the way society's

---

3. See Luke 4:18–19; Acts 1:7–8, 2:32–47.

4. Alister McGrath, *Theology: The Basics* (Oxford: Oxford University Press, 2011), 139.

5. This comes down to the question of whether we believe what is prayed in the Lord's Prayer is actually possible. A Wesleyan framework allows and calls us to believe it is.

structures of class, race, and political affiliation divide the church. Rather than the four approaches explained above, a Wesleyan approach finds the theological declaration of the church's oneness tied to the church's own responsibility to work with "unwearied patience" for unity.[6] Thus, the church's unity is not just descriptive. It is normative and imperative. In other words, we do not sit back and try to discern the church's unity through different lenses. We act proactively to create a church unified. In fact, this "unwearied patience" is also true of the church's holiness, catholicity, and apostolicity.

The Church's Holiness

The church's holiness is grounded in its identity as the people of God. The story of God's people extends back to God promising Abraham a nation that will be a blessing to all peoples of the earth (Gen. 12:2–3). This promised nation, or peoplehood, throughout the Old Testament is Israel. Israel (as a collection of people) is considered holy because they are chosen by God. In the New Testament, we find that God's chosen peoplehood is indeed opened to all peoples of the earth through the life, death, and resurrection of Jesus and the offering of the Holy Spirit. God's people are no longer limited to an ethnicity or particular land. God's new covenant includes all who respond willingly to being God's called-out people in the world. In fact, the word in the New Testament that is commonly translated as "church" is *ecclesia*, which literally means "the called out." The church is the new covenant people of God, so the church is holy.

Stating that the church is chosen by God can sound as if Christians are given a status of prestige in the world. However, inherent in this chosenness is the call to "regard others as better than yourselves" (Phil. 2:3, NRSV), and follow in the way of Christ Jesus,

> who, though he was in the form of God, did not regard equality with God as something to be exploited, but emptied himself, taking the form of a slave, being born in human likeness. And being found in human form, he humbled himself and became obedient to the point of death—even death on a cross. (Phil. 2:6–8, NRSV)

Being God's chosen is not a status of prestige, but the responsibility for Christian communities is "to be holy and blameless before [God] in love" (Eph. 1:4, NRSV). The church is to take on the role of a servant in the world, humbly and obediently, just as Christ did.

Admittedly, the church has not always lived fully into this call. Christians in various traditions today recognize sin in their own communities, as well as their own personal ability to desire the ways of the world rather than the way of

---

6. Wesley, "Of the Church," in *Works*, 3:55.

Jesus. Rather than representing holiness and wholeness, the church often reveals its own brokenness. However, the church is only able to truly recognize and confess its sin *as* sin and its idolatry *as* idolatry because of the formational grace it receives through worshiping God and through relationships of mutual accountability by the people of God.[7]

As John Wesley clarifies, there is an ongoing repentance and faith that is necessary in the Christian life, personally and communally for the "continuance and growth in grace"[8] toward holiness. The church is empowered by the Spirit to be continually transformed toward the way of Jesus Christ and the love of the Trinity; as the church lives in holy covenant with the triune God, it expresses that holiness in the world through love. Paul claims without reservation that the church in Corinth (of all places!) is holy. In the next breath he says, now *become* what you are. (See 1 Cor. 1:2 and 2 Cor. 7:1.)

The Church's Catholicity

When we acknowledge that the church is "catholic" (or universal), we admit that God's peoplehood is not limited to a single congregation, denomination, movement, or cultural expression of Christian worship. Every Christian is a part of this universal community. More significantly, when we recognize the nature of the church as the Spirit-empowered peoplehood that transcends national and social borders, we acknowledge that all are essential to God's mission and work in the world. The coming reign of God is portrayed in Scripture as "a great multitude that no one could count, from every nation, from all tribes and peoples and languages" surrounding the slaughtered Lamb in worship (Rev. 7:9, NRSV). And as Darrell Guder explains, the church now serves as "the sign, foretaste, firstfruits, and agent of the reign of God that Jesus announced and inaugurated."[9]

The significance of the church universal does not, however, render local gatherings insignificant or less fully church than the universal church. The Spirit who is at work in the church universal is the same Spirit at work in the local gatherings. "There is one body and one Spirit, just as you were called to the one hope of your calling, one Lord, one faith, one baptism, one God and Father of

---

7. See Phillip Kenneson, "Worship, Imagination, and Formation," in *Blackwell Companion to Christian Ethics,* ed. Stanley Hauerwas and Samuel Wells (Malden, MA: Blackwell Publishing, 2004), 63.

8. Wesley, "The Repentance of Believers," in *John Wesley's Sermons,* 406. See also Wesley, "Of the Church," vol. 3 of *Works* B, 55. Wesley explains that the church is called holy because the Head of the church is holy, its "ordinances are designed to promote holiness," and because God "intended that all the members of the church should be holy."

9. Darrell Guder, *Missional Church: A Vision for the Sending Church in North America* (Grand Rapids: Eerdmans, 1998), 76.

all, who is above all and through all and in all" (Eph. 4:4–6, NRSV).[10] The Holy Spirit's work throughout the church transforms every local gathering from simply being a piece of a puzzle to being the very expression of God's work in the whole church.

Perhaps the most difficult aspect of acknowledging the universal church is the contradictory tendency for congregations, traditions, movements, and Christians from different cultures to feel at odds with one another rather than partners in God's mission. John Wesley addresses this in a sermon he distributed titled "On Catholic Spirit." He pleads for the opportunity to join hands and fellowship with people of other Christian traditions and movements. He suggests they practice unity by agreeing on the essentials of Christian faith and making space for diversity and debate in nonessential matters.[11] The following well-known phrase, as repeated by Phineas Bresee, reflects this call for catholic spirit: "In essentials unity, in non-essentials liberty, in all things charity."[12] The church's catholicity is a call for Christian groups to discern their group's contribution to the church as a whole, to learn from each other in love, and to hope together for the fulfillment of the inaugurated reign of God.

The Church's Apostolicity

It is commonly explained that the church is *apostolic* as it passes on the teachings and tradition of Jesus's original apostles. At times this has meant that there is a direct, and thus trustworthy, line of succession (of clergy) from the apostles, particularly Peter, until now. This succession guarantees, then, the fidelity of the faith through the centuries. A more Wesleyan way of understanding this idea is that the church is apostolic because the same Spirit who was at work in the lives of Jesus's original apostles, and in the formation of the church, has continued to be at work among God's people, revealing God's purposes and forming us into faithful witnesses of the gospel. Thus, it is the Spirit who secures the church's faithfulness, rather than a traceable, unbroken line. The church has been given the task of being the community that interprets Scripture in order to continue teaching truth and practice regarding the triune God in a consistent way; continuity is found in the church's ongoing invitation to its members and to the world to place its active trust and hope in this Trinity.

---

10. It is important to note here that John Wesley leans on Ephesians 4:1–6 for his sermon "Of the Church," *Works* 3:45–57.

11. Wesley, "On Catholic Spirit," in *John Wesley's Sermons*, 299–310.

12. See Mark Maddix, "Understanding the Essentials," *Holiness Today*, November/December 2011; see also *The Nazarene Messenger* 5, no. 23 (Dec. 6, 1900): 4. The actual quote has been attributed to Augustine, although many scholars believe it came much later, perhaps from the Lutheran tradition.

The church's apostolicity does mean, then, that the church preserves and passes on the Christian tradition.[13] However, this does not mean that the church passively hands over a stagnant set of doctrines from context to context and generation to generation. Tradition understood in light of the Spirit's active work is much more dynamic than that. Theologian Jaroslav Pelikan offers a helpful definition of *tradition* here. He says, "Tradition is the living faith of the dead; traditionalism is the dead faith of the living."[14] His point is that tradition is often tied to negative connotations because people confuse it with traditionalism. The church as apostolic community does not just teach about what God did in the *past* but also about what God is doing *now*, and finds connecting the two very important. The church is challenged to listen to the Spirit through the ancient documents of Scripture and tradition yet always live in God's joy and hope as the church comes alive contextually in the places and times it presently inhabits. In other words, while the church passes on its teachings and tradition, the church also participates in the discernment of faithful Christian practice and theological thinking relevant for today. (See chapter 3 for more on tradition in the role of the church and theology.)

We believe in one, holy, catholic, and apostolic church. How do we reconcile this belief with the recognition that the church has fallen short of this declaration? First, we must recognize that the church's oneness, holiness, catholicity, and apostolicity is grounded in its identity as *God's* people and the way the Spirit has sustained and continues to sustain the church; we are what we are because God has declared it and God makes it so. Second, we must recognize that inherent in this fourfold declaration is a call for the church to become what it is created to be. All within the church community are responsible to participate and make manifest these characteristics and its purpose. May the Spirit continue to draw us into the holy love of the Trinity so that we may be sent out to the world as the living body of Christ to bear faithful witness to the reign of God.

Discussion Questions

1. How have you thought about the church's oneness before reading this chapter?

2. In what sense is the church holy; in what sense is it not?

3. What kind of responsibility does the church have as the covenanted holy people of God?

---

13. See the following scriptural passages for insight on the apostolic nature of the church: 1 Cor. 15:3; 1 Tim. 6:20; 2 Tim. 2:2; 2 John 9.

14. Jaroslav Pelikan, *The Emergence of the Catholic Tradition (100–600)*, vol. 1 of *The Christian Tradition: A History of the Development of Doctrine* (Chicago: University of Chicago Press, 1971), 9.

4. In what ways have you seen your congregation embrace the universal church?

5. Finish this sentence: If the Spirit who was at work in the lives of the original apostles and the formation of the church is currently at work in the life of the church today, then . . .

Suggestions for Further Reading

Guder, Darrell. *Missional Church: A Vision for the Sending of the Church in North America*. Grand Rapids: Eerdmans, 1998.

Harper, Brad and Paul Louis Metzger. *Exploring Ecclesiology: An Evangelical and Ecumenical Introduction*. Grand Rapids: Brazos Press, 2009.

Leclerc, Diane and Mark A. Maddix. *Essential Church: A Wesleyan Ecclesiology*. Kansas City: Beacon Hill Press of Kansas City, 2013.

Volf, Miroslav. *After Our Likeness: The Church as the Image of the Trinity*. Grand Rapids: Eerdmans, 1998.

seventeen

WHAT IS THE CHURCH'S MISSION?

—❦—

Joshua R. and Nell Becker Sweeden

The word *mission* conjures up many images in the last two centuries of the church. For much of the more modern period, mission represented the church's emphasis and programs to send people to faraway places to proclaim the gospel. Later in the modern period, corporate and organizational models of mission compelled local churches and their leadership to better identify the purpose, vision, and uniqueness of their own communities. In more recent conversation, mission has been a driving concept for what is called *the missional church*, with corollary emphases of *missio Dei* (the mission of God—a more theological field of study) and the *incarnational church* (churches who see their purpose in living like the compassionate Jesus).

Indeed, mission is being re-engrafted into the life of the church and bound to the very identity of what it means to be Christian. And so today, mission still connotes sending, but it also signifies *all* the people of God as being sent. As David Bosch puts it, "Missionary activity is not so much the work of the church as simply the church at work."[1] The rediscovery of how the nature and mission of the church go hand in hand—that "the church is essentially missionary" and its "mission is essentially ecclesial"—has helped to give rise to what is now the missional church movement in North America.[2]

---

1. David J. Bosch, *Transforming Mission: Paradigm Shifts in Theology of Mission* (New York: Maryknoll, 1991), 372.

2. Ibid. See also Guder, *Missional Church*. Guder notes, "It has taken us decades to realize that mission is not just a program of the church. It defines the church as God's sent people. Either we are defined by mission, or we reduce the scope of the gospel and the mandate of the church. Thus our challenge today is to move from church with mission to missional Church" (*Missional Church*, 6).

The World Is My Parish

The critical question for the missional church movement of today is this: What would an understanding of the church (an ecclesiology) look like if it were truly missional in design and definition?[3] While not necessarily the driving motivation for Wesley, the Methodist movement became a key answer to such a question. Wesley found little vibrancy in the faith of believers within the Church of England of his time. He was motivated to renew the church, not primarily through institutional change but through the transformation of people's hearts and lives. This change centered on a commitment to the lifelong call to holiness and the proclamation of a holistic gospel message for the poor and marginalized. Subsequently, Wesley was propelled toward new places and unique ways of organizing his ministry in order to renew the church and extend its mission.

Wesleyan historian Richard Heitzenrater describes John Wesley's journey as one that moved away from traditional parish congregations and toward itinerant ministry. Wesley's open-air preaching and focus on nurturing small groups of Christians ignited the Methodist movement.[4] Interestingly, though Wesley always had a strong discipleship impulse, he was initially unconvinced by the peculiar methods of open-air preaching employed by his friend and fellow minister George Whitefield. Wesley was persuaded, however, when he saw thousands flock to listen and seek transformation under Whitefield's preaching. Seeing the response to open-air preaching as a sign of the movement of the Spirit, Wesley also began preaching on the streets, in front of buildings, and in public squares. Wesley was convinced that his calling and ordination made it necessary for him to overstep parish boundaries and traditional ministerial protocol in order to fulfill God's commission to preach the gospel.[5] Wesley affirms his discernment of God's calling on his life in his often-quoted statement: "I look upon *all the world* as my parish; thus far I mean, that in whatever part of it I am, I judge it meet, right, and my bounden duty to declare unto all that are willing to hear the glad tidings of salvation."[6]

---

3. Guder, *Missional Church*, 7.

4. Open-air preaching or itinerant preaching was also identified as field preaching, but this is often a misnomer because Wesley was not necessarily preaching in fields but in strategic, open-air locations within a town or city, where he could be seen and heard. These locations included graveyards—where Wesley preached atop tombstones—market squares, or in front of large trees or buildings that would amplify the sound of his voice. See Richard P. Heitzenrater, *Wesley and the People Called Methodists* (Nashville: Abingdon Press, 1995), 100.

5. Ibid., 102. Heitzenrater adds: "The local clergy, quite naturally, looked upon these activities of the visiting clergy as unwarranted if not illegal incursions into the parish life of the city" (ibid., 101).

6. Wesley, in *Letters I*, vol. 25 of *Works* B, 616. Heitzenrater, in *The People Called Methodists*, notes that this statement "was the basic rationale that would undergird Methodist itinerancy: God

Yet Wesley knew that success in preaching must be measured by the full conversion of individual hearts and lives. Structures and processes for spiritual formation and discipleship were needed. Accordingly, Wesley established a structure of bands (small groups) and later classes (house meetings) to nurture spiritual growth through confession, prayer, and service.[7] Wesley's understanding of conversion was comprehensive and holistic. He believed "the way of salvation" moved Christians toward a continual journey of "perfection in love, sanctification, or the restoration of the image of God" as the ultimate goal of their lives.[8] Wesley's interest was to nurture believers in response to God's grace, from justification to sanctification. As such, the groups he established were neither exclusive nor elitist. In fact, initial membership only required "a desire to flee from the wrath to come, and to be saved from their sins."[9]

Wesley's vision for the bands and classes hinged on a holistic embodiment of the gospel. As Rebekah Miles puts it, "One could no more be a Christian and refuse to love and care for a neighbor than one could be a Christian and refuse to love God. Indeed, in the end, both loves amounted to one thing—the one happiness and one religion."[10] Wesley encouraged all members to manifest their faith through love—to visit the sick and imprisoned, care for orphaned children and widowed women, and to engage in works of mercy as means of grace in the way of salvation. For Wesley, one's individual transformation would always lead to outward manifestations of social transformation.[11] Christian holiness was social in nature for Wesley, or more specifically, relational in perfect love of God and neighbor.

The bands and classes that would come to be identified with the Methodists were meant to be an *ecclesiolae* within the *ecclesia*—that is, a small church

---

determines the scope of mission and preaching" (102).

7. Wesley's societies were defined as "a company of [people] having the form and seeking the power of godliness, united to pray together, to receive the word of exhortation, and to watch over one another in love, that they may help each other to work out their salvation." John Wesley, "The Nature, Design, and General Rules of the United Societies. General Rules," in *The Methodist Societies: History, Nature, and Design*, ed. Rupert E. Davies, vol. 9 of *Works* B, 69.

8. Rebekah Miles, "Happiness, Holiness, and the Moral Life in John Wesley," in *The Cambridge Companion to Wesleyan Theology*, ed. Randy L. Maddox and Jason E. Vickers (Cambridge: Cambridge University Press, 2009), 210.

9. Quoted in Miles, "Happiness, Holiness, and the Moral Life," 211. Additionally, those *on the way* of salvation were to follow three general rules: (1) do no harm, (2) do good, and (3) attend upon all the ordinances of God. For a good summary of the Methodist guidelines, see David Lowes Watson, "Methodist Spirituality," in *Exploring Christian Spirituality: An Ecumenical Reader*, ed. Kenneth J. Collins (Grand Rapids: Baker, 2000), 186.

10. Miles, "Happiness, Holiness, and the Moral Life," 210.

11. Ibid.

gathering in order to reform the broader church.[12] Wesley's interest was not to create a denomination or even a movement but to revitalize the Church of England. Wesley's impulse for renewal was driven by a desire to see Christians nurtured toward loving God and neighbor wholeheartedly. Here we see the clearest vision of a Methodist understanding of mission: God's calling of all believers toward deeper personal and social holiness is intrinsically tied to the church's calling to minister to the world and nurture Christian faithfulness.

Will Mission Save Us?

Wesley never used so-called *missional* language to describe his concern for the cultivation of holiness or his hope "that the love of God might be shed abroad in [their] hearts and lives."[13] Nonetheless, Wesley's orienting concern and the role of Methodist societies as *ecclesiolae* can speak to the missional impetus of today. It has already been noted that the terms *mission* and *missional* can carry a variety of meanings, so to add missional as a qualifier of the church is not to say much at all. We know Wesley's ministry was motivated by his own powerful experience and confirmation of God's work in his life—often associated with his Aldersgate experience. Yet, as much as his experience of a "heart strangely warmed" drove his sense of mission, his ministry was always grounded in the life of the church—gathering in order to nurture a deeper search for God's holiness and the restoring of humanity.[14] In this regard, the church remained the locus of the transformation of the individual believer, the church, and society.

The contemporary missional church movement appropriately derives its sense of mission from the very nature of the triune God. Bosch dates the more intentional development of the term *mission* to the 1952 Willingen Conference in which theologians unpacked the following: "The classical doctrine on the *missio Dei* as God the Father, sending the Son, and God the Father and the Son sending the Spirit as expanded to include yet another 'movement': Father, Son, and Holy Spirit sending the church into the world."[15] Following this Trinitarian trajectory, the *missio Dei* is revealed as people who are gathered in Christ's name,

---

12. We are indebted to Bryan Stone for illuminating Wesley's radical ecclesial formation through *ecclesiolae* in *ecclesia* in his unpublished paper "Wesleyan Ecclesiology: Part I and II," 2007. Stone draws from Colin Williams's development of these concepts in *John Wesley's Theology Today* (Nashville: Abingdon Press, 1960). Also see Howard A. Snyder, *The Radical Wesley and Patterns for Church Renewal* (Downer's Grove, IL: InterVarsity Press, 1980).

13. Heitzenrater, *The People Called Methodists*, 105.

14. Stone draws out this point nicely in his unpublished essay "Wesleyan Ecclesiology," 4. F. Ernest Stoeffler, "Tradition and Renewal in the Ecclesiology of John Wesley," in *Traditio-Krisis-Renovatio aus Theologischer Sicht*, ed. Berndt Jasper and Rudolf Mohr (Marburg: Elwer, 1976), 309.

15. Bosch, *Transforming Mission*, 390.

conformed to his image, and empowered by the Holy Spirit to reveal the love of God in and for the world. Learning how to be in solidarity with the incarnate and crucified Christ is nurtured and challenged through those called out as *ek-klesia*. Wesley and the early Methodists share a clear affinity for the Willingen Conference explication of mission. As Wesley's own engagement with open-air preaching attests, he saw the Spirit at work in the nontraditional Methodist revival yet maintained the centrality of formation in the church to nurture and nourish Christian faithfulness.

In early Methodism we see an intentional interweaving of the paradoxical relationship between the missional movement and the institutional church that is often absent today. Missional church writers Michael Frost and Alan Hirsch note, "Christology determines missiology, and missiology determines ecclesiology."[16] The value of their statement is in how it reminds Christians to be suspicious of *ecclesiocentrism*—an idolatrous elevation of the church at the expense of God's continued revelation and activity in the world. The danger of their statement, however, is that it can too quickly dismiss the fact that our missiology and Christology do not exist in a vacuum. That is to say, they do not arise out of thin air or on their own. Rather, missiology and Christology are encountered and learned through the church gathered as Christ's body in the world.

The fact that the church is always embedded in specific contexts further demands a more generalized and universal understanding of mission. The modern drive for relevance in the recent past can be seen in emphases on church growth, societal influence, and notoriety. While the more contemporary missional church movement is, in many ways, a critique of this instinct, it is undeniable that mission can still be co-opted and commercialized for the consumer church. How-to literature and seminars on achieving a missional church are symptomatic. Furthermore, when mission becomes aligned with achievement, there is a danger of programming both the church and the movement of the Spirit. The church is seen only for its utility, and the movement of the Spirit becomes a static reflection of our own interests.

Interestingly, the later, modern pattern of making such fads as church growth commodities is precisely the problem that gave rise to the missional church movement in the first place. Thomas Edward Frank rightly notes how even the metaphor of "making disciples" encapsulated in many of our church mission statements can easily become formatted into a canned process so that a disciple begins to sound like a product of the church. And the more disciples a church produces, the more it will grow in numbers, gain notoriety, and win

---

16. See Michael Frost and Alan Hirsch, *The Shaping of Things to Come: Innovation and Mission for the 21st-Century Church* (Peabody, MA: Hendrickson Publishers, 2003), 16.

recognition at the regional meetings among church leaders and pastors.[17] How quickly the church can lose sight of the real mission.

Holiness of Heart and Life: The Wesleyan Way

John Wesley knew there are no shortcuts or quick fixes to Christian formation and faithfulness. As Stanley Hauerwas and William Willimon note, "The only way for the world to know that it is being redeemed is for the church to point to the Redeemer by being a redeemed people."[18] Yet, as the past two thousand years of church history attests, being a redeemed people is no easy task. Wesley refused to be discouraged, though, and recalled the challenging call of the gospel: "But strive first for the kingdom of God and his righteousness, and all these things will be given to you as well" (Matt. 6:33, NRSV). Accordingly, the message of holiness—of *seeking* God wholeheartedly, both individually and corporately—reflects the ongoing task of discovering how God's redemptive activity is shaping a people as a sign of that redemption.

The church in all its manifestations and traditions is called to be reforming as it integrally participates in God's mission in and for the world. Bosch reiterates: "The cross which the church proclaims also judges the church and censures every manifestation of the complacency about its 'achievements.'"[19] The church in the power of the Spirit is an object of the *missio Dei*, but it is not yet a perfect manifestation of the reign of God.[20] Subsequently, the church is in continual need of repentance and conversion as it seeks to point to God's mission by being a redeemed people. This is the impetus behind the Wesleyan renewal movement, but so was the conviction that even the church blunders and struggles with unfaithfulness. Yet by God's grace it remains the anticipation of God's reign and shalom in history, a sign of the new creation to come.[21]

For Wesley, holiness as a lifelong pursuit of the image of God is intrinsically tied to the gathering of the church. The church is more than just a vehicle for the organization of small groups or the awakening of an already imaged holiness instilled in believers. Instead, the church gives shape and coherence to the nature of holiness itself and how the life of holiness is awakened and nurtured. Wesley's understanding of the way of salvation that steers all believers toward an ever deepening holiness of heart and life—not just as individuals but togeth-

---

17. Thomas Edward Frank, *The Soul of the Congregation: An Invitation to Congregational Reflection* (Nashville: Abingdon Press, 2000), 33.

18. Stanley Hauerwas and William H. Willimon, *Resident Aliens: Life in the Christian Colony* (Nashville: Abingdon Press, 1989), 94.

19. Bosch, *Transforming Mission*, 387.

20. Ibid.

21. Ibid., 387–88.

er as God's people strengthening and sharpening one another—*is* our ecclesial mission as we seek to be conformed and reformed to Christ's body in and for the world. After all, "The church's final word is not church but the glory of the Father and the Son in the Spirit of liberty."[22] Holiness is about *reflecting* God, not *being* God; this is our mission.

Questions for Discussion

1. In light of John Wesley's emphasis on the holistic embodiment of the gospel, how is your local congregation called to live out God's mission in its community?

2. What are the *ecclesiolae*, or small forms of church, that helped to reform the broader church in Wesley's day? What might be new forms of *ecclesiolae* that help renew the church today?

3. How has *mission* been co-opted in our society today? In what ways is the church's embodiment of mission a testimony to God's restoration of all creation?

4. How is the call to holiness also a call for the church to fulfill God's mission? What does this look like in the church of the twenty-first century?

Suggestions for Further Reading

Bosch, David. *Transforming Mission: Paradigm Shifts in Theology of Mission.* Maryknoll, NY: Orbis, 1991.

Guder, Darrell L., ed. *Missional Church: A Vision for the Sending of the Church in North America.* Grand Rapids: Eerdmans, 1998.

Snyder, Howard A. *The Radical Wesley and Patterns for Church Renewal.* Downers Grove, IL: InterVarsity Press, 1980.

Wesley, John. "John Wesley's Discourses on the Sermon on the Mount." In *John Wesley's Sermons: An Anthology*, edited by Albert Outler and Richard Heitzenrater. Nashville: Abingdon Press, 1991.

---

22. Jurgen Moltmann, *The Church in the Power of the Spirit* (Minneapolis: Fortress Press, 1977), 19, quoted in Bosch, *Transforming Mission*, 377.

eighteen

HOW DO WE VIEW PEOPLE
OF OTHER RELIGIONS?

———— ◦≪◦ ————

Kelly Diehl Yates

Wesleyans, along with other Christians, believe that every person is born in sin and that, because we are sinful, we cannot have a relationship with the triune God unless God intervenes. Wesleyans also believe that even though we are born in sin, God gifts everyone with prevenient grace when we are born. This prevenient grace answers the question, *How can persons who are full of sin even understand that God desires a relationship with them?*

Prevenient literally means "before," and prevenient grace is the grace that goes *before* our saving relationship with God or even our understanding of the love of God. Prevenient grace has several functions for Wesleyans. It is a function of prevenient grace that "all truth is God's truth" and that Christians and non-Christians alike have access to general knowledge in the world. (For example, a Christian does not have deeper knowledge of how the brain functions than does an atheistic neurosurgeon!) Further, Wesleyans believe that God gives prevenient grace at birth to every person. It is prevenient grace that keeps children and the disabled in the loving arms of God, until they can, if possible, be held accountable for their sins. Prevenient grace also functions in understanding how persons become Christian. Prevenient grace is what draws or woos every person toward God. Salvation thus begins with prevenient grace. God's prevenient grace provides even the first inclination to please God and the first conviction of sin.[1] Prevenient grace provides us with the ability to respond to God's offer of salvation through Jesus Christ. Wesley describes the work of prevenient grace with

———————————

1. Wesley, Sermon 85, "On Working Out Our Own Salvation," in *Sermons III*, vol. 3 of *Works* B, 203.

examples of God drawing people to hear God's Word, sometimes out of simple curiosity, but Wesley would say that *even* that curiosity is God's prevenient grace at work. Wesley attributes a person's conscience to prevenient grace. Any good choice—any choice for peace, love, kindness, or compassion before a person accepts Christ as Savior—only happens because God has offered prevenient grace. Wesley taught that it was impossible for a non-Christian to love another person without the prevenient grace of God.

Wesley understood prevenient grace as providing us with an ability to respond to God's offer of salvation, but he also recognized prevenient grace as providing us with the idea of what it means to be a human being.[2] In a letter he wrote in 1776, Wesley asserts that no person is without prevenient grace.[3] Wesley did not see people as trying to earn the grace of God but as *already* graced by God simply because they are human. He described the grace of God as "free for all" as well as "in all."[4] Thus the idea of a person without grace is purely hypothetical for Wesley.

The concept of prevenient grace also helps answer a very difficult question. Do persons who have not heard of Christ have any hope of eternal salvation? One of the foundations of Wesleyanism is the belief that all people have the potential for a saving relationship with God. While we believe that God can and does save people in a moment of faith in Christ, we also hold out hope for those without that opportunity. Because of God's prevenient grace in their lives, people are always being drawn into relationship with God. Wesleyans believe that *everyone* is in this process, no matter the circumstances or religion. Put simply, God never gives up on anyone. Everyone's salvation is dependent on whether he or she has lived up to the light he or she has received—if a person has not received the light that explicitly knows of Christ as Savior, God will judge that person accordingly. But for the purposes of this chapter, the emphasis will not be on the response of persons to God, but on our response to them. Since we believe that every person is created by God in the image of God, and we believe that all persons are graced by God through prevenient grace, in a sense we view them as God's people: God loves all the children of the world.

As Wesleyans we believe that we can love others because God first loved us. Since God values people, we value people—because God has given them prevenient grace, we do not view them as hopeless. This belief provides us with guidance in our view of people who practice other religions, a guidance that can be shown with optimism, humility, and coexistence.

---

2. J. Gregory Crofford, *Streams of Mercy: Prevenient Grace in the Theology of John and Charles Wesley* (Lexington, KY: Emeth Press 2010), 94.

3. Wesley, *Letters* 6:239.

4. Wesley, Sermon 110, "Free Grace," in *Sermons III*, vol. 3 of *Works* B, 544.

Optimism

If we choose to focus on *people* who practice other religions rather than on the *religions* they practice, then we can see people through the eyes of grace. Wesley describes this as "unspeakable tenderness," by which we long for the welfare and not destruction of others.[5] A Wesleyan view of humanity is optimistic because we believe every person is capable of a relationship with God because of the grace God already provides. Wesley preached that God in God's mercy holds the *life* of an individual to be of greater importance than that individual's *ideas*.[6] Ideas provide a framework for systems of belief, and the definition of religion is a system of belief. People are not valued by God because of their systems of belief but simply because God made them. Because God made them, God offers them prevenient grace.

Humility

If we choose to look back on our lives and see God's prevenient grace at work, we can be convinced that it is only by the grace of God that we stand where we are today. We can look at others and see God at work in multiple ways—even people who practice other religions. No person has the authority to condemn another to eternal judgment. There is nothing in the New Testament that teaches Christians to present themselves as better than others. In fact, 1 Peter 2:12 instructs, "Conduct yourselves honorably among the Gentiles, so that, though they malign you as evildoers, they may see your honorable deeds and glorify God when he comes to judge" (NRSV). *Gentile* refers to those who are not Jewish, but it can also be interpreted today as those who live outside the will of God.

In an end-of-life sermon preached in 1790, Wesley claimed that no one has the right to sentence "all the heathen [meaning those with no religion] and Mahometan world [an eighteenth-century description of Muslims]" to hell.[7] He left the judgment to God. Since God made the so-called heathen and Mahometan, then God provides them also with prevenient grace. If God provides them with prevenient grace, then we have an obligation to see them as God's children who will be judged on the basis of how they have lived up to the light they have received (see Rom. 2). If we see them as people God desires and loves, we can work together toward the common good. In 1 John 4:19, we read, "We love because he first loved us." In humility we accept that we are God's children and that only through the love of God, who sent Jesus Christ, can we love anyone else.

---

5. Wesley, Sermon 39, "Catholic Spirit," in *Sermons II*, vol. 2 of *Works* B, 95.
6. Wesley, Sermon 106, "On Faith," in *Sermons III*, vol. 3 of *Works* B, 499.
7. Wesley, Sermon 130, "On Living Without God," in *Sermons IV*, vol. 4 of *Works* B, 174.

Coexistence

If we choose to see people who practice other religions as graced by God in the same way that we believe ourselves to be, then we can work with them for the common good, and we can even coexist. Coexistence may be defined as living peaceably with each other as a matter of *policy*, or guiding principle. As Wesleyans, our policy of prevenient grace leads us to our policy of respectful coexistence.

Wesley probably did not encounter many people who practiced religions other than Christianity. Yet his theology seems to point to a practice of coexistence not found among many Christians of his time. In a sermon in 1749, Wesley refers to Mark 9:38–40, where the disciples want Jesus to stop the men who are not Jesus's own disciples but are casting out demons in Jesus's name. Wesley, listing many groups who are not Christian, says that if Christians forbid these groups from "casting out devils," then they are bigots. If *we* forbid groups who are not Christian from "casting out devils," then Wesley would deride us as well.

But one could ask, "What if the other group does not allow *me* to coexist?" There are many countries that do not allow Christians to practice their religion openly; the reigning power does not allow coexistence. Wesley addresses this in a sermon where he ends with the plea never to return evil for evil. We must remember our Lord Jesus, who preached, "Love your enemies and pray for those who persecute you." When the religious groups of his day refused to allow Jesus to coexist with them, they arrested and killed him; he did not in any way retaliate. If we live by the command of Jesus, we will never return evil for evil.

In the sermon "The General Spread of the Gospel," Wesley quotes Isaiah 11:9 (KJV), "The earth shall be full of the knowledge of the LORD, as the waters cover the sea." After describing the sin of the present day, he says, "Such is the present state of mankind in all parts of the world! But how astonishing is this, if there is a God in heaven, and if his eyes are over all the earth! Can he despise the work of his own hand?"[8] This means Wesley thought that one of the main reasons the gospel was not advancing was due to *absence* of love and forbearance in the lives of Christians. If Christians would live as God intended them to live, then the loving knowledge of God, producing uniform, uninterrupted holiness and happiness, would cover the earth, "and fill every soul."[9] Wesley was able to let God be God, instead of trying to judge the eternal destiny of people.

Wesley's struggle reflects the voice of God in Hosea 11:8–9 (NRSV):

How can I give you up, Ephraim? How can I hand you over, O Israel? How can I make you like Admah? How can I treat you like Zeboiim? My heart recoils within me; my compassion grows warm and tender. I will not

---

8. Wesley, Sermon 63, "The General Spread of the Gospel," in *Sermons II*, vol. 2 of *Works B*, 495.

9. Ibid.

execute my fierce anger; I will not again destroy Ephraim; for I am God and no mortal, the Holy One in your midst, and I will not come in wrath.

We advance the love of God when we coexist. Instead of judging, we should leave that role to God. Wesley believed that the greatest stumbling block to the spread of the gospel is Christians not living out love toward everyone, even those who disagree with them. When we show love by coexisting with others because we believe they have received God's gift of prevenient grace, we advance the gospel of Jesus Christ. Why would anyone ever be drawn to a hateful and bigoted faith?

Wesleyans believe God has the power to convert the whole world. What if we allowed God to lead us to act in kindness instead of judging those who practice other religions? What if, instead of condemning, we offered a hand of friendship and worked together in communities to bring about peace? Perhaps then we would live in the kingdom Jesus preached. Rather than viewing different religions as purely satanic that must be extinguished by Christianity, a Wesleyan view of prevenient grace sees God at work in everyone and sees other religions as a hopeful expression of those who seek God.

Discussion Questions

1. When you look back on your life, how do you see prevenient grace as drawing you toward God?

2. How would your perspective change if you made a conscious effort to perceive God at work in the people around you every day, no matter their faith professions?

3. What interfaith groups exist in your city? How could you learn more about other religions in order to work toward a greater understanding with real people you know?

4. How can Christians reach out in friendship to Jews and Muslims? What can your church do specifically to bring peace in your community?

Suggestions for Further Reading

Crofford, J. Gregory. *Streams of Mercy: Prevenient Grace in the Theology of John and Charles Wesley.* Lexington, KY: Emeth Press, 2010.

Lodahl, Michael. *Claiming Abraham: Reading the Bible and the Quran Side by Side.* Grand Rapids: Brazos Press, 2010.

Meadows, Philip R. "Candidates for Heaven: Wesleyan Resources for a Theology of Religions." *Wesleyan Theological Journal* 35, no. 1 (Fall 2000): 99–129.

Yates, Kelly Diehl. "The Wesleyan Trilateral: Prevenient Grace, Catholic Spirit, and Religious Tolerance." *Wesleyan Theological Journal* 48, no. 1 (Spring 2013): 54–61.

Young, Amos. "A Heart Strangely Warmed on the Middle Way? The Wesleyan Witness in a Pluralistic World." *Wesleyan Theological Journal* 48, no. 1 (Spring 2013): 7–27.

nineteen

HOW WILL IT ALL END?

---∽∾∾---

Charles W. Christian

Eschatology is a term built upon the Greek word *eschaton*, which means "last" or "final," and speaks to the conclusion of history in terms of God's purposes and goals. *Telos*, the Greek word for "goal," is used frequently in the study of eschatology.

Army helicopters, suddenly abandoned cars, panic, and chaos: These are the popular images associated with eschatology, or, last things. Best-selling books and mainstream movies packed with well-known movie stars are filled with these images, all purporting to tell the story of the culmination of all things in accordance with God's ultimate goals.

However, Christianity's earliest discussions of last things take a decidedly different approach. The book of Revelation, written in largely symbolic, apocalyptic language, was originally intended to assist believers to overcome and to be encouraged, even during times of harsh oppression and persecution so that the ultimate triumph of Jesus Christ and his ways would be revealed to all (see Rev. 2:7 and 3:5, for example). We find a sense of excitement and blessing, along with a sense of expectation (the time is near), instead of the sense of fear and dread often associated with popular Christian and non-Christian perceptions of Revelation and of eschatology in general.

The study of eschatology addresses both individual and corporate dimensions. Individually, eschatology addresses the full realization of the fellowship with God engendered by salvation (initial sanctification) and entire sanctification. Individual eschatology informs us about the full experience of the goal (*telos*) of the saving relationship provided through the work of Jesus Christ. This includes questions about death, the time between death and the second coming of Christ, and the ultimate destiny of both believers and unbelievers when Christ returns.

Corporately, eschatology addresses the transition between the community who walks by faith—which is the church universal (the body of Christ in the world)—and the church glorified, who will experience in full what their work throughout history has sought to foreshadow. This community of believers joins with all of creation in expectation of the ultimate triumph of God's ways (see Rom. 8:22). Corporate aspects of eschatology address how the new and glorified creation will function for all eternity.

Historical Eschatology

Like all Christians, Wesleyans have particular lenses through which we see God's future culmination of all things. First, though, it would be helpful to gain an overview of ways in which Christians have traditionally viewed eschatology. These three differing paradigms, which use Revelation 20:1–8 (a description of the millennial reign of Christ) as a key text, are summarized as follows:

1. The kingdom of God is largely in the future.

Some Christians view biblical references to the consummation of God's purposes—such as Revelation 20—as referring to events mostly in the future, long after the biblical writers and their audiences could have understood the full impact of their writings.

For church fathers like Irenaeus, the present reign of God was difficult to discern. Therefore, the culmination of all things to the glory of God was seen as more futuristic, something that is to come later in history. Justin Martyr, a second-century Christian writer, interpreted the Revelation passage as demonstrating "two advents of Christ" and a literal thousand-year reign of Christ in an expanded Jerusalem.[1] This view later came to be known as *premillennialism*. This approach sees the coming of Christ as something that will happen before (*pre*) the actual, literal millennial reign of Christ on earth.[2]

While many versions of this premillennial approach have emerged throughout the centuries, a version of premillennialism that has become most notable in popular circles is known as *dispensational premillennialism*, or simply, *dispensationalism*. This view posits that there will be a literal (not symbolic) thousand-year reign of Christ, on the earth, in the future, before the final judgment. In fact, the extremely literal reading of the symbols in the book of Revelation and elsewhere in the Bible leads this group to argue that there will be two distinct comings of Jesus Christ: one in the air at the rapture and the second with the church at the beginning of this millennial kingdom.

---

1. Justin Martyr, "Dialogue with Trypho," in *The Apostolic Fathers, Justin Martyr, Irenaeus*, trans. Marcus Dods and George Reith, ed. Alexander Roberts, James Donaldson, and A. Cleveland Coxe, vol. 1 of *Ante-Nicene Fathers* (Buffalo, NY: Christian Literature Publishing Co., 1885). See an extended discussion on the history of millennialism in James Leo Garrett, Jr., *Systematic Theology: Biblical, Historical, and Evangelical*, vol. 2 (Grand Rapids: Eerdmans, 1999), 750–51.

2. Versions of this view are also called *chiliastic*, based on the Greek word for "thousand."

According to this view, God has allowed history to unfold in seven "dispensations," or eras, of grace, in which God deals with and even tests human beings differently in the context of each era.[3] For dispensationalists, the role of the church is parenthetical because the true climactic event of all of history is yet to come: It is the second coming of Jesus Christ. A more radicalized dispensational approach seeks to make apocalyptic/symbolic references so literal that one can actually predict the time of the second coming based on its clues, despite the fact that Jesus himself warns against such an attempt (Matt. 24:36).[4] While premillennialism has had a long history in the church, dispensationalism is actually a fairly recent invention. Some of its theology has been questioned. If not careful, it can tend toward modalism (a Trinitarian heresy) and place the church as secondary to God's concern for the Jews.

2. The kingdom of God is to be realized fully before Jesus comes.

A view that was popular in John Wesley's day, and that Wesley and many of his contemporaries held, is known as *postmillennialism*. Evangelism, according to this view, would help bring about the reign of God and the return of Christ by transforming both individuals and society at large in such a way that fulfills the purposes of God before Christ ultimately returns to rule and reign. It is not accidental that the popularity of this view coincided with revolutions of democracy, the beginnings of the Industrial Revolution, and the overall rise in literacy and education.[5] By the twentieth century, two world wars, the Great Depression, and the rise of weapons of mass destruction, among other things, accompanied the near disappearance of postmillennialism.

3. The kingdom of God is present among us yet awaits its full realization.

Other approaches to Revelation 20 see the millennial reign of Christ on earth as symbolic rather than literal and as associated specifically with the presence of the Holy Spirit working in and through the church. *Amillennialism*, strongly associated with Augustine in the fourth century, sees the reign of Christ as visible now in the work of the church of Jesus Christ on earth. The end of this symbolic millennium will be the second coming of Christ, which will occur

---

3. For a detailed discussion of nine distinctive elements of dispensational theology, see Garrett, *Systematic Theology*, 2:756–57.

4. See, for instance, Hal Lindsey, *The Late Great Planet Earth* (Grand Rapids: Zondervan, 1970), a best-selling book in the 1970s, brought dispensationalism to the forefront. Recent proponents of this view include Tim LaHaye's 16-vol. *Left Behind* series (Carol Stream, IL: Tyndale, 1995—2007) and the works of popular television preacher John Hagee.

5. For a brief introduction to postmillennialism, see Dale Moody, *The Word of Truth* (Grand Rapids: Eerdmans, 1981), 553–55.

at the end of history as we know it. It will consist of a final judgment and final resurrection.

Eschatology Through Wesleyan Lenses

It is important to note that Wesleyan denominations have not traditionally had an official millennial view regarding eschatology. However, there are key paradigms that emerge in a Wesleyan approach to last things.

1. The kingdom is here now and will be fully realized later.

For Wesley, the goal of entire sanctification is not simply personal holiness but, rather, deeper participation in the kingdom of God. As Diane Leclerc states, for Wesley, entire sanctification is possible due to "God's desire to work through us."[6] Furthermore, initial sanctification (salvation) and entire sanctification move toward ultimate sanctification—the glorification of those who have been redeemed and the fulfillment of the promise of deeper and eternal fellowship with God.

Eternal life, according to Scripture, does not begin when Christ returns but, rather, when a person believes in and follows Jesus Christ (John 3:16–18). The words of Christ proclaiming that "the kingdom of God is among you" suggest that we are currently experiencing the kingdom of God because we are experiencing the presence of God through the power of the Holy Spirit. We as believers do not wait for the coming of the kingdom. Rather, through service of Christ, through participation in the sacraments, and through the sharing of the gospel, we demonstrate that the kingdom *has* come in the person and work of Christ and that its full realization is *yet* to come in God's own time and by God's own hand.

2. The last days are about a Person, not a calendar.

Indeed, Jesus himself in a real way *is* the embodiment of last things. He is the final Word spoken to us "in these last days," in the words of Hebrews 1:2. He is present in what 1 John 2:18 calls (speaking of the biblical writer's own time) the "last hour." Jesus, then, as theologian Adrio Konig reminds us, was not born in the middle of history, nor was he born as part of the story line leading up to the climax of history. Rather, Jesus Christ *is* the climax of God's history for God's creation.[7] This means the kingdom of God—though fully realized when "every eye will see" Jesus face to face (Rev. 1:7)—is present now, and the last days are already upon us. This fact is not intended to be a source of dread but a source of

---

6. Diane Leclerc, *Discovering Christian Holiness* (Kansas City: Beacon Hill Press of Kansas City, 2010), 281.

7. Adrio Konig, *The Eclipse of Christ in Eschatology* (Grand Rapids: Eerdmans, 1989). Konig's assertion has become a classic modern example of this approach to eschatology.

hope and comfort, since the one who ushered in the last days with his birth is walking with us in the power of the Holy Spirit. He will also reveal himself fully—this "full unveiling" is the idea behind the word *parousia* in the New Testament, which is often translated as "second coming." Soon, all of creation, which groans for his appearing (Rom. 8:22) will become the full embodiment of what God has desired since the beginning of creation.

3. God's goal is transformation, not escape.

As Wesley stated in a sermon called "The New Creation," physical transformation is God's ultimate goal and is the logical working out of the plan of salvation and sanctification God has in mind for us.[8] Wesleyans join with believers throughout Christian history in affirming the "resurrection of the body," and not the Platonic escape from the body into spirit-beings that has often captured the attention of popular (and, sadly, some of Christian) culture.[9] Furthermore, we echo Wesley's emphasis upon the care of all of God's creation, not because we worship creation but because, as theologian Stan Grenz reminds us, "The old will give way to something radically new. Yet it is *this* cosmos that God will transform into the new creation."[10]

Eschatology, then, is not the escape from our created bodies into an ethereal, spiritual existence but is, rather, a demonstration of the power of the resurrection first embodied in Jesus Christ, whose resurrected body could be touched and seen. Furthermore, our eternal home is not an ethereal realm that replaces a destroyed, original creation. Rather, it is a beautifully transformed picture of all creation fully redeemed by the love and grace of God after death, suffering, and sin have been ultimately vanquished.[11]

4. Eschatology is about optimism, not pessimism.

For Wesleyans, God's timeline for last things is not about clinging tightly to small billows of hope as we brace ourselves for unthinkable destruction and chaos. Rather, it is about drawing present hope from the risen Christ, who—because he has given us his Spirit (John 14)—allows us, even in the midst of promised suffering and persecution, to see the victory of God now and in the days to come.

---

8. A more detailed discussion on this sermon and its implications can be found in Maddox, *Responsible Grace*, 236–38.

9. This idea is noted clearly in the creeds of the church. See the Apostles' and Nicene Creeds. Karl Barth's short book *Dogmatics in Outline*, trans. G. T. Thompson (London: SCM Press, 1949), contains extended discussion of the resurrection of the body as a key Christian paradigm.

10. Stanley J. Grenz, *Theology for the Community of God* (Nashville: Broadman and Holman, 1994), 842–43.

11. For further discussion, see N. T. Wright, *Surprised by Hope* (San Francisco: Harper One, 2008).

This is the reason for our optimism and the reason we need not dread reading and talking about last things. Indeed, Scripture reminds us that every time we partake in the Eucharist (the Lord's Supper), we "proclaim the Lord's death until he comes" (1 Cor. 11:26). We celebrate the cross and the resurrection of Jesus, which is a present reality in these last days, in anticipation of when the full reality of that resurrected life is unveiled (the *parousia*) for all creation to experience and witness.

This optimism does not mean we ignore teachings regarding hell and judgment. Indeed, Wesley himself held a literal view of hell as a place of eternal separation from the love of God and of terrible punishment.[12] It is part of the working out of the purposes of God, who—though desiring that all be saved (1 Tim. 2:4)—lovingly allows God's own creation to reject and partially thwart aspects of God's overall goals for redemption.

All of this leads to a view of Jesus Christ and his love as central to eschatology, just as it is to all other aspects of Wesleyan theology. Jesus Christ is the climax of God's redemptive history. All else is what literature calls the *dénouement*—the portion of the story in which the climax is fully worked out and its ramifications fully realized and experienced.

When the fully realized aspect of the kingdom of God appears, all fears will be vanquished, and the fullness of the love and peace of God—which came into full view in the person and work of Christ—will be fully realized. The old will be completely gone, and the love of God will be completely unveiled. And "he [Jesus Christ] shall reign for ever and ever" (Rev. 11:15, KJV). At last!

Discussion Questions

1. How can a more optimistic view of last things affect our approach to the study of last things in the Bible?

2. In what ways does Wesley's emphasis upon sanctification help us see the kingdom of God as a current, not just a future, phenomenon?

3. How does the optimism of grace found in Wesleyan theology influence our views of judgment and hell?

4. What difference does it make to center our eschatology upon the life and work of Jesus rather than upon events leading up to the second coming of Jesus?

Suggestion for Further Reading

Boone, Dan. *Answers for Chicken Little: A No-Nonsense Look at the Book of Revelation.* Kansas City: Beacon Hill Press of Kansas City, 2005.

---

12. Maddox, *Responsible Grace*, 251–52.

Konig, Adrio. *The Eclipse of Christ in Eschatology*. Grand Rapids: Eerdmans, 1989.

Maddox, Randy L. *Responsible Grace: John Wesley's Practical Theology*. Nashville: Kingswood, 1994.

Wright, N. T. *Surprised by Hope: Rethinking Heaven, the Resurrection, and the Mission of the Church*. San Francisco: HarperOne, 2008.

ABOUT THE SCHOLARS

Editors

Rev. Diane Leclerc, PhD, is professor of historical theology at Northwest Nazarene University and has taught for almost twenty years, receiving the Professor of the Year award in 2015. She has published many articles, chapters, and seven books, including *Discovering Christian Holiness: The Heart of Wesleyan Holiness Theology* (2010) and *Essential Church: A Wesleyan Ecclesiology*, with Mark A. Maddix (2014). She has served as president of the Wesleyan Theological Society and is a member of the Wesleyan-Holiness Women Clergy Association. She pastored a Nazarene congregation in Maine and served as the first pastor of a new church plant in Boise, Idaho.

Rev. Mark A. Maddix, PhD, is professor of practical theology and Christian discipleship and dean of the School of Theology and Christian Ministries at Northwest Nazarene University. He served in pastoral ministries for twelve years and in teaching ministry for more than fifteen years. He has served as the president of the North American Professors of Christian Education. He has published many articles and coauthored five books, including *Discovering Discipleship: Dynamics of Christian Education* (2010) and *Spiritual Formation: A Wesleyan Paradigm* (2011). Mark is a frequent speaker on topics of Christian discipleship, spiritual formation, and online education.

Contributors

Rev. Charles W. Christian, PhD, is an ordained minister in the Church of the Nazarene. His doctorate is in systematic and moral theology, and he is currently senior pastor of the Church of the Nazarene in Cameron, Missouri.

Rev. Benjamin R. Cremer, MA, MATS, received his degrees from Northwest Nazarene University and Nazarene Theological Seminary. He currently pastors Euclid Community Church of the Nazarene in Boise, Idaho.

Rev. Rhonda Crutcher, PhD, has spent her career in Christian higher education. She and her husband have served as Nazarene educational missionaries in both Europe and Africa and currently serve as supporting ministerial staff at Piedmont Church of the Nazarene in Oklahoma. Rhonda is on faculty at Southwestern Christian University in Bethany, Oklahoma.

Dick O. Eugenio, PhD, is a Filipino scholar serving as associate professor of theology at Asia-Pacific Nazarene Theological Seminary in the Philippines. He is also an associate pastor of Taytay First Church of the Nazarene in Manila.

Rev. Timothy R. Gaines, PhD, serves as assistant professor of religion at Trevecca Nazarene University and has authored several articles and books, including *A Seat at the Table: A Generation Re-imagining Its Place in the Church*. He previously served as co-pastor of Bakersfield First Church of the Nazarene in California and hosts a podcast dedicated to the art and craft of preaching called *The Sermon Studio*.

Rev. Joe Gorman, DMin, is associate professor of practical theology and director of the undergraduate online Christian ministry program at Northwest Nazarene University. He is also the executive director of Compassion for Africa, an organization that engages in sustainable, compassionate ministry projects in Africa. Prior to teaching, he served as a senior pastor in Colorado for twenty-one years.

Rev. John Grant, PhD Candidate, is an ordained minister in the Church of the Nazarene. He has served as a pastor in churches in North Dakota and Washington State. He is also an adjunct professor at Northwest Nazarene University and Nazarene Bible College.

Rev. Ryan L. Hansen, PhD, is the lead pastor at Blakemore Church of the Nazarene in Nashville. He has taught as an adjunct professor at Garrett-Evangelical Theological Seminary, Olivet Nazarene University, and Northwest Nazarene University. His book, *Silence and Praise: Rhetorical Cosmology and Political Theology in the Book of Revelation*, was published by Fortress Press.

Rev. Jacob Lett, PhD Candidate, is a visiting lecturer of theology at MidAmerica Nazarene University and an ordained minister in the Church of the Nazarene. His degree will come from the University of Manchester.

Rev. David McEwan, PhD, is the academic dean and director of research at Nazarene Theological College in Brisbane, Australia, his native country. He lectures in theology and pastoral theology, specializing in the thought and practice of John Wesley. David is an ordained minister in the Church of the Nazarene and has pastored churches in the UK and Australia.

Rev. Gift Mtukwa, PhD Candidate, is pursuing his degree in biblical studies through Nazarene Theological College, Manchester. He is on faculty in the religion department at Africa Nazarene University in Nairobi, Kenya.

Rev. Joshua R. Sweeden, PhD, is an ordained minister in the Church of the Nazarene. He is assistant professor and Richard B. Parker co-chair in Wesleyan theology at George Fox Evangelical Seminary and has taught at Eastern Nazarene College.

Rev. Nell Becker Sweeden, PhD, is an ordained minister in the Church of the Nazarene. She is assistant professor and Richard B. Parker co-chair in Wesleyan theology at George Fox Evangelical Seminary. She studied at Boston University for her PhD.

Rev. Eric M. Vail, PhD, is associate professor of theology at Mount Vernon Nazarene University. His prior publications on the doctrine of creation include *Creation and Chaos Talk* (2012) and "Creation out of Nothing Remodeled" in *Theologies of Creation: Creatio Ex Nihilo and Its New Rivals* (2015).

Sarah Whittle, PhD, is a British scholar and part-time lecturer in biblical studies at Nazarene Theological College, Manchester. She is based in St. Andrews, Scotland, where she works at the university in a student welfare role. She is the author of *Covenant Renewal and the Consecration of the Gentiles* with Cambridge University Press, 2015.

Rev. Montague R. Williams, PhD Candidate, is assistant professor of religion and philosophy at Eastern Nazarene College. He served in youth and family ministry for ten years prior to teaching. He has several published articles and book reviews, and regularly leads workshops and retreats that examine intersections between theological ethics and congregational life.

Celia I. Wolff, ThD Candidate, studied Christian Scripture and ethics at Duke Divinity School. She presently serves as assistant professor of New Testament at Northwest Nazarene University.

Rev. Kelly Diehl Yates, PhD Candidate, is a student of Wesley studies at Nazarene Theological College, Manchester. She teaches at Southern Nazarene University in Bethany, Oklahoma, and has served the Church of the Nazarene in pastoral ministry for fifteen years.